Costa Rica Travel Guide 2023

The Most Complete Pocket Guide to the Wonders of Costa Rica | Discover History, Food, Folklore, and Unmissable Wilderness of the Land of Happiness

By
Mike J. Darcey

© Copyright 2023 - All rights reserved.

The content contained within this book may not be reproduced, duplicated, or transmitted without direct written permission from the author or the publisher.

Under no circumstances will any blame or legal responsibility be held against the publisher, or author, for any damages, reparation, or monetary loss due to the information contained within this book. Either directly or indirectly.

Legal Notice:

This book is copyright protected. This book is only for personal use. You cannot amend, distribute, sell, use, quote, or paraphrase any part, or the content within this book, without the author's or publisher's consent.

Disclaimer Notice:

Please note the information contained within this document is for educational and entertainment purposes only. All effort has been executed to present accurate, up-to-date, and reliable, complete information. No warranties of any kind are declared or implied. Readers acknowledge that the author does not render legal, financial, medical, or professional advice. The content within this book has been derived from various sources. Please consult a licensed professional before attempting any techniques outlined in this book. By reading this document, the reader agrees that under no circumstances is the author responsible for any direct or indirect losses incurred due to the use of the information contained within this document, including, but not limited to, errors, omissions, or inaccuracies

Table of Contents

Introduction 4

Chapter 1: Planning Your Trip 6

What to pack..7

Tips on how to budget for your trip and how long to stay..9

Money-saving advice.. 11

How To Get Around Costa Rica................................... 12

Available Modes Of Transport...................................... 12

Here are few bus stops to take note of: 14

Best tips to help you appreciate Costa Rican culture, food, natural sights, and customs like a local.......... 15

Chapter 2: Things You Must Know about Costa Rica... 18

System of justice 19

Tips to avoid legal pitfalls on your trip..................... 20

Currency and ATMs tips.. 21

Common Spanish Phrases to know. 23

Insider tips... 28

Chapter 3: Places to visit and Activities......... 30

Some Hidden gems... 66

Costa Rica Wildlife 69

Activities to do as a family during a trip to Costa Rica 73

Chapter 4: Itineraries 76

3 days itinerary.. 80

five days itinerary.. 81

7 days iterary.. 83

Two weeks itinerary.................................... 86

Chapter 5: Where To Stay 90

Hostel La Posada - Affordable, Friendly, Beach Vibes 91

Tranqui Funkey Cabinas.............................. 92

Chapter 6: Costa Rica Cuisine and Restaraunts... 94

Chapter 7: Entertainment And Nightlife In Costa Rica.. 98

Nightlife In Costa Rica...............................100

Chapter 8: Shopping and Souvenirs in Costa Rica 103

Souvenirs 104

Conclusion 107

Introduction

Welcome to Costa Rica! This little Central American nation is well recognized for its stunning natural beauty, rich culture, and welcoming people. It is located between Nicaragua and Panama to the south.

You can discover rocky mountains, deep jungles, and sandy beaches all close by in Costa Rica, a country of contrasts. Over 500,000 different plant and animal species may be found in the nation, which is home to an astonishing variety of flora and fauna. Around 25% of Costa Rica's total land area is made up of national parks and reserves, many of which are found there.

The first residents entered the region some 3,000 years ago, beginning a lengthy and rich history for the nation. Native Costa Ricans lived in complex communities and left behind a number of significant cultural items, such the petroglyphs in the province of Guanacaste and the stone spheres in the Diquis Delta.

The Spanish colonized Costa Rica in the sixteenth century, bringing with them their language, religion, and way of life. The majority-Roman Catholic nation of Costa Rica's official languasge is Spanish. There are many different cultures and practices coexisting in Costa Rica due to its diverse population.

A long history of stability and social advancement has earned Costa Rica a reputation as a peaceful, democratic nation. It is renowned for its dedication to environmental protection, with several programs in place to safeguard the nation's natural resources.

Chapter 1: Planning Your Trip

Planning a trip to Costa Rica can be enjoyable and fulfilling, but it's important to do your research and make sure you have everything you need before leaving. The following should be considered while you plan your trip:

Best Time to Visit Costa Rica Considering the Weather and High Tourist Seasons

Costa Rica is a year-round vacation location with plenty to do every season. However, depending on where you go and what you want to do, the weather and tourist seasons can vary greatly. Based on the weather and the busiest travel times, here are some recommendations for when to visit Costa Rica:

Dry season: The dry season, which lasts from December to April, is the ideal time to visit Costa Rica.

The weather is frequently colder and drier in the Central Valley and sunny on the coast, making it the ideal time to go to the beach, go hiking, or partake in other outdoor activities. The peak travel season falls during the dry season, thus costs will be higher and there will be more travelers.

Wet season: From May through November, the wet season is often more humid and rainier, with afternoon downpours occurring more frequently. Due to the rain's role in nourishing the nation's profusion of greenery, the wet season is often referred to as the "green season." If you want to travel during the off-season to avoid crowds and pay less, keep in mind that some outdoor activities can be hampered by the rain.

Optimum time to go: There is no one optimum time to visit Costa Rica; it depends on your interests and what you want to accomplish. If you prefer outdoor activities and beach vacations, the dry season can be excellent for you. If you want to avoid the crowds and pay less, the wet season can be a great option.

The average high temperature in Costa Rica is between 77- and 81-degrees Fahrenheit (25 and 27 degrees Celsius). However, the country does offer a variety of microclimates, with variations in temperature and humidity based on altitude and proximity to the coast. It's a good idea to check the weather prediction before your trip and pack appropriately.

What to pack

The tropical environment and erratic weather of Costa Rica should be taken into account when packing.

Following is a list of what to bring depending on the weather:

- Pack light, loose-fitting clothing made of natural fibers like cotton or linen that is breathable. T-shirts, tank tops, shorts, skirts, and sundresses are all appropriate choices. Lightweight apparel will keep you comfortable in Costa Rica's sometimes-sweltering humidity.
- Rain gear: It's important to take a lightweight rain jacket or poncho because Costa Rica sees rain all year long. Think about wearing sandals or footwear that is waterproof. Having a tiny travel umbrella is also beneficial.
- Swimwear: Be sure to bring your swimwear! Bring a swimsuit or a pair of swim trunks since Costa Rica has many options for swimming and lovely beaches.
- Sun protection: Bring lots of sunscreen (preferably one with a high SPF), a broad-brimmed hat, sunglasses, and lightweight long sleeves for further sun defense in Costa Rica.
- Use insect repellent: In Costa Rica, particularly in the tropical areas, mosquitoes and other insects are prevalent. To prevent bites, bring an effective insect repellent that contains DEET or a natural option like citronella oil.
- Comfortable shoes: If you intend to explore national parks or engage in outdoor activities, bring a pair of durable walking shoes or hiking boots. For informal outings and trips to the beach, flip-flops or sandals are perfect.
- Light layers are advised because, despite Costa Rica's typically warm climate, there may be

some regional and altitude-related temperature differences. For cooler evenings or higher altitude locations like Monteverde or Arenal, bring a lightweight sweater or jacket.
- When going on day trips or treks, a daypack or small backpack will come in handy for carrying necessities like water, snacks, sunscreen, insect repellant, a rain jacket, and a camera.
- Bring a travel adapter if your electrical equipment have multiple plug types so you can charge them in Costa Rica's Type A and Type B power outlets.
- Personal things and medications: If you take prescription drugs, make sure to pack enough of them. Additionally, it's wise to bring anypersonal hygiene items you prefer or might not find easily in Costa Rica.

Remember to check the weather forecast for the specific regions you plan to visit in Costa Rica as conditions can vary. Additionally, consider the activities you have planned, such as hiking or visiting the rainforest, and pack accordingly.

Tips on how to budget for your trip and how long to stay.

Budgeting: Although Costa Rica is typically less expensive than many other nations in the region, it's still crucial to plan your spending wisely to ensure you have enough money to meet all of your expenses. Depending on your vacation preferences and the activities you wish to undertake, prices can vary, but a general idea of your budget might include:

Flights: Depending on your departure location and the season, round-trip airfare from the US to Costa Rica can cost anywhere from $300 to $800 or more.

Accommodations: The cost of hotels and vacation rentals in Costa Rica fluctuate widely, but you can typically find something that is within your means. Budget motels frequently start at around $30 per night, while more luxury lodgings may cost up to $100 per night. Vacation rentals, which can include apartments or homes, can be a great alternative for families or groups and start at less than $50 per night.

Transportation: Buses and shuttles are readily available between major cities and tourist destinations in Costa Rica's efficient public transportation system. These can range in price, but a one-way ride should cost between $10 and $20. Renting a car, which will run you between $40 and $60 per day, is something you might want to think about if you want to explore more of the nation.

Activities: Depending on what you wish to do, Costa Rica offers a vast variety of activities with a wide range of rates. While entrance fees to national parks and other attractions might range from $10 to $20, a guided tour or adventure sport like rafting or zip-lining can cost anywhere from $50 to $100 or more.

Budgeting for meals, mementos, and other incidentals is also a good idea. By eating at neighborhood restaurants and markets and buying at neighborhood shops and markets, you can save money. Additionally, since not all places accept credit cards, it's a good idea to have extra cash on hand just in case.

Overall, it's wise to budget carefully and plan ahead to ensure that you have enough money to meet all of your costs while in Costa Rica. You can stretch your budget and make the most of your trip by doing some homework and comparing costs. Having a backup strategy is also advisable in case of unforeseen costs or emergencies. To protect yourself from trip cancellations, medical problems, and other unforeseeable circumstances, think about getting travel insurance. Additionally, keep in mind that sometimes the best memories are those that result from unplanned detours and impromptu excursions.

Money-saving advice

Costa Rica is one of the most expensive countries in Central America. Fortunately, there are several ways to save money while you're here. Some of the most effective ways to cut expenditures in Costa Rica include the ones listed below:

- Travel during the off-season: Prices are normally lower and fewer people are usually present during the so-called "rainy season," which lasts from late April to November. If you're on a tight budget, go there.
- Avoid group tours; there are many fantastic (but pricey) group excursions offered across the country. Spend your time swimming, hiking, and relaxing at the beach instead.
- Eat at the sodas: "Sodas" are affordable, family-run restaurants that emphasize regional food. A dinner at a soda typically costs around 3,500 CRC. These neighborhood restaurants often have the most affordable prices in the whole country.

- Go camping: Many hotels and hostels will allow you camp on their grounds if you have a tent. Normally, 6,000 CRC is required for each night.
- To experience the country's splendor without having to pay the hefty prices of the well-known Pacific sites, visit the less expensive Caribbean side.
- Despite being substantially slower and less expensive than the tourist buses, they should be avoided. If you're not in a rush, use the neighborhood buses.
- carry a water bottle. A water bottle with a purifier might enable you to save money by purifying the tap water for you (and thousands of plastic bottles).

How To Get Around Costa Rica

There are many entertaining and fascinating things to do and attractions to visit in Costa Rica. To visit the stunning nation, you'll need to find a trustworthy and comfortable form of transportation. Your travel costs might be cut by being aware of the best possibilities.

Available Modes Of Transport

There are many different ways to get about Costa Rica. To get about Costa Rica, there are airlines, taxis, buses, and automobile hire services/rental cars. It's up to you to choose the mode of transportation that best suits your needs in Costa Rica because costs are typically reasonable.

1. Buses

The cheapest mode of transportation in Costa Rica is the bus. Practically all of the nation's bus services are located in San Jose. Bus fare ranges from $4 to $13 for medium- to long-distance travel.

One of the well-known bus services is Goflito, which needs reservations in advance and issues tickets with specific travel dates and seat numbers. It is possible to travel without making reservations, but for these types of transportation services, it is best to always reserve your tickets ahead of time. Additionally, when making reservations in advance, confirm that the travel dates listed on your ticket are accurate. Even if the error wasn't your fault, you won't be able to change or get a refund for your tickets in these situations. Additionally, roundtrip tickets are not available, so if you want to avoid disappointment, make sure to purchase a return ticket as soon as you get at your destination.

The most comfortable buses are those operated by Ticabuses, which have air conditioning, comfy seats, enough legroom, and decent luggage capacity.

Keep note of the schedules for Costa Rican buses because they are known to alter regularly.

2. Car

Renting a car will serve you well in Costa Rica if you want control over your transportation. Purchasing a vehicle is another option.

Finding out whether you require an international driver's license is vital, but if you are from the UK, US, or Canada, you can drive in Costa Rica with a valid driver's license.

On signage on the surface of the road, the speed limit is frequently indicated. The normal highway speed limit is between 75 and 90 kilometers per hour. The speed limit is reduced to 25 kph to 40 kph in construction zones. Traffic violations, such as failing to use a seatbelt, running a red light, or using a cell phone while driving, are punishable by steep fines called multas. You may be fined $400 or more for certain traffic violations. If you are caught speeding, be prepared to pay up to a $575 fine as they are frequently issued.

3. Motorcycles and Bicycles

To ride a motorcycle around Costa Rica, you will need a motorcycle license. One of the most practical and straightforward methods to go around is on a motorcycle. In the smaller seaside communities, a modest motorbike may be rented for about $70.

Cycling is a great way to move around in Costa Rica because the country's terrain was designed for it. If you have the nerve to drive, be ready to avoid potholes, other drivers, and occasionally cattle.

4. Taxis

Taxi drivers are required by law to utilize marias, the taximeters used in Costa Rica. However, it's normal to come across taxis that don't have meters, especially in San Jose, and fares are negotiated beforehand.

Colectovos are multi-passenger taxis, and the fare from point A to point B is frequently under $0.50. Despite being less popular, they are a very cost-effective mode of transportation.

Here are few bus stops to take note of:

- San José: The "Terminal de Transportes de San José" is the city's primary bus terminal and

serves as a center for numerous bus companies that offer routes around the nation.
- The "Terminal de Buses de La Fortuna" is the bus terminal that is nearest to La Fortuna.
- Manuel Antonio: The "Quepos Bus Terminal" in the neighboring town of Quepos is the closest bus station.
- Santa Elena Bus Terminal is the bus station that is most convenient for Monteverde.
- The "Puerto Viejo de Talamanca Bus Terminal" is the closest bus station in Puerto Viejo.

Keep in mind that getting to some attractions from the bus stops may require additional transportation, such taxis or shuttles. Planning your route ahead of time and researching the most current transportation choices for your specific locations are always wise decisions.

Best tips to help you appreciate Costa Rican culture, food, natural sights, and customs like a local.

Here are some recommendations for experiencing Costa Rican culture, cuisine, natural attractions, and customs like a local:

- Adopt a "Pura Vida" lifestyle: "Pura Vida" is a catchphrase that means "pure existence" in Costa Rica. It captures the relaxed and upbeat mood of the locals. Accept this outlook and approach your encounters with a laid-back, receptive attitude.
- Try Typical Costa Rican Dishes: To fully experience Costa Rica's flavors, try some of the regional fare. The typical dishes gallo pinto

(rice and beans), casado (rice, beans, meat or fish, and side dishes), ceviche (raw fish marinated in citrus juice), and variously prepared plantains are some of the must-try foods. Don't forget to drink a cool cup of horchata or a rich cup of Costa Rican coffee with your dinner.

- Visit crowded markets like Mercado Central in San Jose or neighborhood farmers' markets to experience the lively atmosphere and find fresh produce, spices, and locally made crafts. Ask questions, interact with the sellers, and learn about local culture.
- Play Outside: Costa Rica is known for its breathtaking natural beauty. To fully experience the nation's lush jungles, immaculate beaches, and diverse fauna, partake in outdoor activities like hiking, zip-lining, surfing, or snorkeling. Utilize national parks like Manuel Antonio, Arenal Volcano, or Corcovado to get a close-up look at the nation's biodiversity.
- While many locals in tourist destinations understand English, learning a few basic Spanish phrases will help you communicate with them and demonstrate your interest in their culture. Simple salutations and expressions like "Hola," "Gracias," and "Por favor" (please) will be greatly welcomed.
- Respect the Environment: Costa Ricans hold their natural surroundings in the highest regard, and you should too. Follow the approved pathways, don't litter, and respect the wildlife when you travel responsibly. Think about assisting groups and campaigns

that protect the environment and Costa Rica's natural resources.
- Check the local calendar to see which events and celebrations are scheduled to take place while you are there. Costa Ricans enjoy celebrating, and these occasions provide visitors a chance to see their rich culture, including music, dance, and traditional attire. Participate in the celebrations and get acquainted with the regional traditions.
- Interact with Locals: Have a discussion with locals to learn about their culture and way of life. People from Costa Rica are renowned for being kind and friendly. Don't be hesitant to start conversations and solicit advice. They may have insider knowledge on restaurants, attractions, and cultural experiences that you won't find in tourist guides.
- Stay in Eco-Lodges or Homestays: To experience Costa Rican culture more authentically, think about staying in eco-lodges or homestays. These lodging options offer chances to meet locals, gain personal knowledge about their traditions, and promote eco-friendly travel methods.
- Learn about the history and culture of Costa Rica: Spend some time learning about the culture, traditions, and history of the nation. To learn more about the cultural legacy and the factors that have shaped Costa Rican identity, visit museums, cultural institutions, or go on guided tours.

Chapter 2: Things You Must Know about Costa Rica

Geography: Its northern and southern boundaries are formed by Nicaragua and Panama, respectively. Central America is where Costa Rica is situated. San José, Alajuela, Heredia, Cartago, Puntarenas, Guanacaste, and Limón are its seven provinces. It covers around 51,000 square kilometers in total (19,700 square miles).

The three primary geographical areas that make up the country's varied topography are the Central Valley, the Caribbean Coast, and the Pacific Coast. The Central Valley, where San José, the country's capital, is situated, is the region with the most people. It stands out for having a moderate climate and is well-known for its coffee plantations and fertile land.

The country's easternmost region, the Caribbean Coast, is renowned for its gorgeous beaches and hot, tropical environment. Contrarily, the Pacific Coast is famed for its surf breaks and national parks and has a dry, tropical climate.

Culture: The population of Costa Rica is diverse and influenced by indigenous, Spanish, African, and Asian cultures. Although Spanish is the official language of the nation, English is extensively spoken in tourist regions.

With several festivals and celebrations held throughout the year, Costa Rica has a vibrant cultural history. The annual National Day parade, which honors the nation's independence and takes place on September 15th, is likely the most well-known of these.

People from Costa Rica are renowned for being kind and easy back, and the idea of "pura vida" (pure life) is a significant aspect of the nation's culture. It alludes to the notion of leading a straightforward, laid-back, and stress-free life.

System of justice

The Código Penal de Costa Rica and the Código Procesal Penal, as well as extra particular legislation, apply to both Costa Ricans and foreigners who commit crimes on its territory.

After an arrest, police will detain you. You cannot be held for more than 24 hours without a court order. Usually, only the prosecutor has the power to issue a detention order. The authorities seize the person's entire personal property, including their travel documents, during the arrest. You will be informed of your rights, which include the following.

- to view the warrant obtained against you, learn the reason for your detention, and learn the name of the officer who made the request.
- to quickly notify the individual or organization of your choice that you have been taken into custody.
- to have a lawyer of your choosing represent you from the outset of the proceedings, or in the absence of that, a public defender.
- to be informed of the acts you are accused to have committed and to be submitted to the prosecutor (from the prosecutor's office or Ministerio Pblico) or the court (tribunal).
- to avoid speaking. In the event that you want to speak out, you have the right to do so in the presence of your attorney and are free from any techniques or methods that might be used to coerce, manipulate, or violate your free will or diminish your dignity.
- Not to be subjected to any restrictions on your freedom of movement except from those imposed by the prosecutor or the court.

Tips to avoid legal pitfalls on your trip.

Follow local laws: Familiarize yourself with local traffic laws and follow them to avoid getting into trouble or putting yourself in danger.

Use reputable transportation companies: Choose reputable transportation companies and avoid using unlicensed or unregulated transportation options.

Stay alert: To avoid mishaps or other dangers, stay vigilant and aware of your surroundings when driving.

Follow safety guidelines: Follow safety guidelines and heed warning signs while traveling and be prepared for emergencies.

Practical Information for Travelers, Such As Currency, Language, and Important Phone Numbers

Currency: The colon is Costa Rica's recognized unit of money (CRC). Currency exchange services are provided by banks, companies that exchange currencies, and a few hotels. In tourist locations, the majority of major credit cards are accepted, but it's typically a good idea to bring some cash as well. Before your travel, it's a good idea to become familiar with the exchange rate.

It is a given that you are used to paying with local money in Costa Rica. Understand how much something costs in colones using your own currency. It's important to understand how much you owe and how much change you are entitled to. 500 CRC are equated to $1 US. Having a currency converter app on your phone is a good idea.

Currency and ATMs tips

There are a few guidelines you may adhere to in Costa Rica when it comes to currency conversion and using international ATMs in order to avoid hefty costs and reduce the possibility of illegal activity. Here are a few suggestions:

- Use local currency: The Costa Rican colón is the nation's legal tender (CRC). Even though

some establishments might accept US dollars, it's usually preferable to use local money to avoid negative conversion rates.
- Studying exchange rates Check the exchange rates between your own money and the Costa Rican colón before to your travel. This can help you find fair exchange rates when exchanging money and give you an idea of what to anticipate.
- Money exchange in renowned locations: The best places to exchange currency are trustworthy banks, registered currency exchange locations, or your hotel. Avoid exchanging money on the street or with strangers who might offer better rates but might also be involved in fraud.
- If you need to exchange money, examine the exchange rates and fees provided by several banks or exchange agencies. It's wise to browse around for the greatest bargain because some places might impose more fees or provide less favourable rates.
- Before leaving for Costa Rica, let your bank and credit card provider know about your vacation. This makes it more likely that your cards will function abroad and lowers the possibility that your transactions will be marked as suspicious.
- Use ATMs in trusted locations: Make sure you only use ATMs in trusted, well-known areas like banks, malls, and respectable hotels. Avoid using freestanding ATMs in remote locations as they may be more prone to fraud, such as card skimming.

- Watch out for card skimming: When utilizing an ATM, look for any indications of tampering, such as missing or suspiciously attached parts. To stop covert cameras from recording your information, cover the keypad with your hand while you enter your PIN.
- Select ATMs carefully: Use ATMs that are associated with your bank or have agreements with significant international banks whenever possible. By doing this, you can reduce transaction costs and currency conversion expenses.
- Think about utilizing a travel card: It may be practical to use prepaid travel cards or debit cards made expressly for overseas travel. Look for cards that provide favorable exchange rates, cheap fees, and high levels of security.
- Maintain a cash reserve: Always keep some emergency cash in a secure location, apart from your primary savings. This can be helpful in the event of ATM failures, card loss, or unforeseen circumstances.

Language: Although Spanish is the official language, English is extensively spoken in tourist areas. Knowing a few fundamental words and phrases in Spanish is always useful, such as "hola" (hello), "gracias" (thank you), and "por favor" (please). Speaking the language will be appreciated by many locals, and it might be helpful in more rural or remote locations where English might not be as widely spoken.

Common Spanish Phrases to know.

Beer = Cerveza

Do you speak English? = ¿Hablas Inglés? (Inglés is another cognate!)

Doctor = Medica / Medico (another cognate!)

Food = Comida

Good morning = Buenos días

Good afternoon = Buenos tardes

Good night = Buenos noches

How much does it cost? = ¿Cuánto cuesta?

I don't speak Spanish = No hablo Español

I need = Yo necessito (another cognate!)

I want = Yo quiero (pronounced "yo kee-ero")

Nice to meet you = Mucho gusto

Now = Ahora (silent "h," so it is pronounced "a-ora")

Please = Por favor

Thank you = Gracias

Ticket = Boleto (airplane, train, bus)

Water = Agua (pronounced "ag-wah")

Where is the bathroom? = ¿Dónde está el baño?

You're welcome = De nada

Hola - Hello

¿Cómo estás? - How are you?

De nada - You're welcome

Lo siento - I'm sorry

No entiendo - I don't understand

¿Dónde está...? - Where is...?

Quisiera... - I would like...

¿Puede ayudarme? - Can you help me?

¿Qué recomienda? - What do you recommend?

La cuenta, por favor - The bill, please

¿Dónde está el baño? - Where is the bathroom?

Me gustaría reservar una habitación - I would like to book a room.

¿A qué hora es...? - What time is...?

Phone numbers: Costa Rica's country code is +506.

Here are some important phone numbers in Costa Rica:

1. Tourism Information:
   - Costa Rica Tourism Board (ICT): 800-TURISMO (800-887-4766)
   - Tourist Police (Policía Turística): 2586-4597

2. Government and Administrative Services:
   - Immigration Office (Dirección General de Migración y Extranjería): 1311
   - Civil Registry (Registro Civil): 1311
   - Social Security (Caja Costarricense de Seguro Social): 800-800-8000

3. Embassy and Consulate Numbers:
   - United States Embassy: +506-2519-2000
   - Canadian Embassy: +506-2242-4400
   - British Embassy: +506-2258-2025

- Australian Embassy (located in Mexico City, Mexico): +52-55-1101-2200
4. Transportation:
    - Juan Santamaría International Airport (SJO) - General Information: +506-2437-2400
    - Daniel Oduber Quirós International Airport (LIR) - General Information: +506-2668-1010
    - Public Bus Information (Empresa de Transporte Público de Costa Rica): 2586-4287
5. Other Important Services:
    - Directory Assistance: 113
    - National Water and Sewer Institute (Instituto Nacional de Acueductos y Alcantarillados): 800-ASADAS (800-272327)
    - Poison Control Center (Centro de Información y Control de Envenenamientos): +506-2223-9676 or 2224-7261

Emergency numbers: Costa Rica has several emergency numbers that you should be aware of in case of an emergency. The main emergency number is 911, which can be called for any type of emergency. The number for the Red Cross is 128, and the number for the police is 133. It's a good idea to have these numbers programmed into your phone before your trip.

Vaccinations: Costa Rica does not have any mandatory vaccination requirements for travelers. Some recommended vaccinations for Costa Rica include hepatitis A and B, measles, mumps, and rubella (MMR), and influenza.

Time zone: It is located in the Central Standard Time (CST) zone, which is one hour later than Eastern Standard Time (EST). In Costa Rica, there is no Daylight-Saving Time.

Electricity: Costa Rica uses the same type of electrical outlets as the United States, so you won't need a converter if you're coming from the US. The frequency is 60 Hz, and the usual voltage is 110V. If you're coming from a country with a different voltage or frequency, you'll need a converter and/or transformer.

Drinking water: If you're concerned about the quality of the tap water, you can buy bottled water at most stores and supermarkets.

Tipping: Tipping is not expected in Costa Rica, but it's always appreciated. If you receive good service, it's customary to leave a small tip of around 10% at restaurants and hotels. You can also tip your tour guide or other service providers if you feel they have provided excellent service.

Shopping: Costa Rica has several souvenir shops and artisan markets where you can buy local crafts and products. Food markets are a great place to find traditional Costa Rican dishes and ingredients. The Central Market in San José is a popular destination, with stalls selling everything from fresh produce to handmade crafts. Other markets to visit include the Feria Verde in San José, which sells organic and locally grown foods, and the Mercado Central in Heredia, which specialized in crafts and handmade items.

Safety: Don't leave your valuables unattended and be cautious of pickpockets in crowded areas. It's also a good idea to familiarize yourself with local laws and customs to avoid any misunderstandings.

If you encounter any problems while in Costa Rica, you can seek assistance from the local police or the Ministry of Foreign Affairs. The US Embassy in Costa Rica is in San José and can provide assistance to US citizens, including help with lost or stolen passports, emergencies, and legal issues.

Insider tips

Insider tips and advice from locals and experienced travelers can be a valuable resource when planning a trip to Costa Rica. Here are some tips and advice from locals and experienced travelers on how to avoid tourist traps and find hidden gems in Costa Rica:

- **Avoid tourist traps:** To avoid tourist traps, try to get off the beaten path and explore lesser-known destinations. Avoid areas that are heavily marketed to tourists and instead, seek out local neighborhoods and small towns where you can experience authentic Costa Rican culture.
- **Seek out local recommendations:** Ask locals for recommendations on where to go and what to do. Locals can often provide valuable insights on the best places to visit and the most authentic experiences.
- **Try local restaurants:** Instead of dining at tourist-oriented restaurants, seek out local restaurants and food markets to try authentic Costa Rican cuisine. Local restaurants and markets often offer the best and most affordable food options.

- **Visit national parks and reserves:** Costa Rica is home to several national parks and reserves, which offer opportunities to experience the country's natural beauty and wildlife.
- **Explore the country's different regions:** Costa Rica is a small country, but it has a wide range of landscapes and cultures to explore.

Chapter 3: Places to visit and Activities.

Costa Rica is a magnificent nation renowned for its diverse wildlife, breathtaking natural scenery, and outdoor adventure options.

Here are the top destinations in this nation that you simply must see.

1. Arenal Volcano

It is situated in the northern part of the country, adjacent to the town of La Fortuna, in the Arenal Volcano National Park. One of Costa Rica's most active volcanoes, Arenal Volcano once attracted a lot of tourists due to its regular eruptions. Visitors take part in activities including zip-lining through the nearby rainforest, wildlife spotting, hiking, and visiting hot springs. The surrounding hamlet of La Fortuna became a major destination for visitors to the volcano. Every day, including weekends and holidays, the park is often open. It's crucial to remember that weather and volcanic activity might restrict access to specific park sections, so it's advised to look up advisories or closures before your trip.

2. Monteverde Cloud Forest Reserve

It is a well-known protected area in Costa Rica's Puntarenas province. It is one of the most well-liked ecotourism sites in the nation and is renowned throughout the world for its extraordinary biodiversity and distinct ecology of cloud forests.

Key characteristics:

Biodiversity: A staggering variety of plant and animal species can be found in the Monteverde Cloud Forest Reserve. It has more than 2,500 plant species, many of which are ferns, orchids, and bromeliads.

Ecosystem of the cloud forest: A distinct variety of tropical forest known as a "cloud forest" is distinguished by a high level of humidity, a lingering cloud cover, and an abundance of epiphytes (plants that grow on other plants). A wide and diversified range of plant and animal life can be found in the cloud forest because to the constant moisture given by the clouds. The reserve is even more mysterious and beautiful because of the cloudy atmosphere it creates.

Canopy Tours: Visitors to the Monteverde Cloud Forest Reserve can take canopy tours to view the forest from a distinctive vantage point. These excursions often involve moving across a number of zip lines and suspension bridges that let you glimpse the forest from above while walking amid the treetops. It's a thrilling adventure that provides breathtaking panoramic views and the opportunity to witness wildlife up close.

Hiking and nature routes are available in the reserve, allowing tourists to take a stroll in the cloud forest. The complexity of these trails varies, making them suitable for both novice and experienced hikers.

Conservation initiatives: The Monteverde Cloud Forest Reserve is steadfastly dedicated to sustainability and protection. It was founded in 1972 by a collection of Quaker families who understood the value of preserving the distinctive ecosystem of the cloud forest. The reserve serves as an example of ecotourism that is sustainable and actively encourages study and research to raise public awareness of environmental problems.

Other Attractions: In addition to the reserve itself, the Monteverde area offers various other attractions and activities. The Santa Elena Cloud Forest Reserve is close by and provides similar sensations. There are also butterfly gardens, hummingbird galleries, and frog exhibitions where you can learn more about the region's diverse wildlife.

Visiting the Monteverde Cloud Forest Reserve is a remarkable experience that provides an opportunity to immerse yourself in the beauty of nature and witness its incredible biodiversity. It's a must-visit destination for nature enthusiasts, birdwatchers, and anyone seeking an unforgettable ecotourism adventure.

3. Manuel Antonio National Park

It has the following notable characteristics:

- Location: The park is located in the Puntarenas province, 132 kilometers (82 miles) southwest of San José, the country's capital.
- Biodiversity: it is one of Costa Rica's smallest parks. It is home to an amazing variety of plant and animal species. It includes a range of environments, such as mangrove swamps, rainforests, and stunning white-sand beaches.

The park is home to 184 different bird species and over 109 different mammal species, including monkeys, sloths, iguanas, toucans, and others.

- Beaches: The stunning beaches include Playa Espadilla Sur and Playa Manuel Antonio, to name only two. Beautiful waters that are perfect for swimming, sunning, and relaxing are offered by these stunning beaches. While enjoying the beach, it's important to respect park rules and keep an eye out for animals.
- Hiking Trails: The park has a number of well-kept hiking routes that wind through the rainforest, letting visitors explore the diverse flora and fauna. Two well-liked trails that provide expansive views of the nearby jungle and the shoreline are the Main Trail (Sendero Principal) and the Cathedral Point Trail (Sendero Punta Catedral).
- Observation of Wildlife: It is renowned for its close encounters with wildlife like monkeys and sloths. Hiring a certified guide will increase your chance of seeing wildlife and tell you more about the park's ecosystem.
- The park's visitor amenities, which include picnic spots, restrooms, and a visitor center, are kept in good condition. The visitor center offers details on the ecology, animals, and conservation initiatives of the park. Additionally, authorized tour companies outside the park's entry provide guided tours and pursuits including kayaking, snorkeling, and canopy tours.

- Conservation initiatives: The preservation of Costa Rica's natural heritage depends heavily on Manuel Antonio National Park. It is a component of the wider Central Pacific Conservation Area, which strives to save the ecosystems of the area and enhance eco-friendly travel. To protect the park's delicate habitats and species, tough rules have been put in place.

It's crucial to abide by the Manuel Antonio National Park's rules and regulations when visiting, such as not feeding any wildlife, sticking on approved routes, and properly discarding of litter. Visitors can contribute to preserving the park's natural beauty for future generations by doing this.

4. Tortuguero National Park:

It is renowned for its rich species and stunning natural landscape, making it one of the nation's most well-liked eco-tourism attractions.

Here are some details and salient characteristics of Tortuguero National Park:

- Location: Located in Limón Province, Tortuguero National Park has a total size of about 77,032 acres (31,174 hectares). It encompasses both terrestrial and aquatic regions and reaches along the Caribbean coast.
- Biodiversity: A staggering variety of plant and animal species can be found in the park. It is renowned for having a diverse bird population of about 300 species, including toucans, herons, and kingfishers. The park also serves as a vital nesting area for a number of sea turtle species, including the critically endangered green turtle and the enormous leatherback turtle.
- Protected Marine Environment: It is home to a vast network of canals and lagoons in addition to a significant stretch of the coastline. The wider Tortuguero Conservation Area, which includes mangroves, marshes, and coral reefs, attempts to safeguard the park's unique marine ecosystems. These waterways are a component of that area.
- Turtle Nesting: The chance to see sea turtles lay their eggs and hatch their young is one of Tortuguero National Park's key draws. Many species of turtles visit the park's beaches to lay their eggs, including green turtles, leatherback turtles, hawksbill turtles, and loggerhead turtles. During the nesting season, guided excursions are offered at night, giving guests the chance to see this amazing natural phenomenon.
- Viewing Species: Tortuguero National Park is home to a wide range of wildlife in addition to turtles. There is an opportunity for visitors to

see wildlife including caimans, howler monkeys, capuchin monkeys, sloths and river otters. Jaguars live in the park as well, though they are not frequently spotted due to their elusiveness.
- Ecotourism Activities. These pursuits include kayaking, hiking through the park's paths, and excursions for birdwatching. Guided boat cruises through the park's canals are also on the list. Visitors have a choice of lodging alternatives when staying in or close to the park thanks to neighborhood eco-lodges.
- Tortuguero National Park is a key player in the effort to preserve Costa Rica's natural heritage. It is managed by the National System of Conservation Areas and is under government protection (SINAC). The park's delicate ecosystems are protected, sustainable tourism practices are encouraged, and scientific research and education are supported.

To make the most of your experience if you intend to visit Tortuguero National Park, it is advisable to review the specific policies and instructions supplied by the park administration as well as the optimum time to see sea turtle hatching.

5. Corcovado National Park

The renowned Corcovado National Park is located on the Osa Peninsula in southwest Costa Rica. It is considered to be one of the places with the highest biological diversity on the globe and is sometimes referred to as the "crown jewel" of Costa Rica's national park system. The following information about the park:

- Biodiversity: The astounding variety of plant and animal species found in Corcovado National Park is unmatched. Approximately 2.5% of the world's biodiversity is thought to reside in the park. Several ecosystems, including lowland rainforest, cloud forest, mangrove swamps, and coastal regions, can be found within its borders.
- Wildlife: A number of endangered species can be found in the park. It is one of the few locations in Central America where these secretive big cats can be located due to its number of jaguars. Tapirs, scarlet macaws, white-faced capuchin monkeys, spider monkeys, sloths, and a variety of reptiles and amphibians are some other notable species.
- Trails & hiking: Corcovado has a vast network of trails that let tourists explore its many different landscapes and get up close to its abundant animals. There are short, pleasant strolls as well as longer, harder excursions on the paths. San Pedrillo, Los Patos, and Sirena are a few well-liked trails. A professional guide is strongly advised due to the park's challenging geography and thick forest, it's crucial to mention.
- In the center of Corcovado National Park, there is a research station and ranger station called Sirena Biological Station. It provides minimal lodging for overnight guests and serves as a hub for experts researching the park's biodiversity. You can fully experience

the park and increase your chances of seeing wildlife by staying at Sirena.
- Corcovado National Park is essential to safeguarding Costa Rica's rich natural heritage. The park is actively managed to protect the preservation of its delicate ecosystems, earning it UNESCO World Heritage status. It also supports environmentally friendly tourism by giving people the chance to enjoy the park with the least amount of negative environmental impact.
- Information for visitors and access: You must plan transportation to one of the park's gates, such as Puerto Jimenez or Drake Bay, in order to visit Corcovado National Park. From there, you may plan tours with a guide or walks in the park. It's crucial to organize your vacation in advance and set up meetings with regional tour guides or park authorities.
- Conservation Obstacles: Corcovado has a number of conservation obstacles, just like many other protected areas across the world. These include poaching, deforestation, illicit hunting, and climate change. These problems are being addressed by stepping up law enforcement, including the community, and using sustainable management techniques.

Experiencing Costa Rica's natural splendor and taking in its astounding diversity of plant and animal life is made possible by Corcovado National Park. Those who love the outdoors and are concerned about conservation should go there.

6. Poás Volcano National Park:

Poás Volcano National Park is a well-liked tourist site in Costa Rica's Alajuela Province. One of the most active volcanoes in the country goes by the name of Poás Volcano. Details about Poás Volcano National Park are provided below:

- Location: The park is around 30 kilometers northwest of San José, the country's capital. There are about 65 square kilometers of it.
- the Poas Volcano The Poás Volcano, which is located in the national park and has an elevation of 2,708 meters, is its main draw (8,885 feet). It is one of Costa Rica's biggest and most active volcanoes. The volcano's crater, which has a circumference of over 1.7 kilometers (1.1 miles) and a depth of 300 meters, is one of the biggest in the world (984 feet).
- Natural Features: The spectacular natural beauty of the national park is well-known. Its beautiful cloud forests, dense vegetation, and variety of plant and animal species are its defining features. The Laguna Caliente (Hot Lagoon) volcano crater lake, which frequently

displays shifting hues owing to volcanic activity, dominates the park's topography.

- Trails and Visitor Center: The park features a well-designed visitor center that offers details on the volcano, its past, and the local ecosystem. The park has a number of hiking routes that allow tourists to experience its unique flora and animals. One of the pathways leads to an overlook from where guests may see the crater of the volcano in its entirety.
- Volcanic Activity: The volcano occasionally releases gases and vapor, which gives the area a surreal atmosphere. This is due to the volcano's active nature. For safety considerations, however, access to the crater may be limited while volcanic activity is at its peak.
- Parking facilities are available for visitors, and Poás Volcano National Park is easily reachable by road. Popular day trips from San José and other adjacent towns go there.
- Facilities for Visitors: The park offers amenities like restrooms, picnic spots, and a small café where guests can eat and drink. Considering that the park's higher elevation can cause lower temperatures, it is advised to pack warm clothing.

It is crucial to seek out the most recent information on volcanic activity, accessibility, and safety precautions from local authorities or park officials before making travel arrangements to Poás Volcano National Park.

7. Tamarindo

The Costa Rican Pacific coast is home to the town and beach resort of Tamarindo. It is located in the Guanacaste province and is well-known for its stunning beaches, surf places, and energetic environment. Tamarindo's breathtaking natural beauty, pleasant climate, and wealth of outdoor activities have made it a popular tourist destination.

Tamarindo's main draw is its expansive, golden-sand beach, which provides ideal conditions for swimming, sunbathing, and a variety of water activities. Tamarindo has consistently good waves that are suited for both novice and expert surfers, which contributes to the sport's popularity there. Those hoping to catch some waves may easily find surf schools and board rentals.

In addition to surfing, Tamarindo provides a variety of other activities like kayaking, scuba diving, snorkeling, and sport fishing and variety of wildlife at the nearby Tamarindo Wildlife Refuge.

Additionally, Tamarindo features a bustling town center with a wide variety of stores, eateries, bars, and nightclubs. Visitors may take in the exciting nightlife, browse the local markets, and eat delicious seafood. The town has a wide variety of restaurants serving both native Costa Rican cuisines and cuisine from other countries.

Tamarindo has a variety of lodging alternatives, from high-end resorts to inexpensive hotels, so there is something to fit any traveler's tastes. The town is a convenient and delightful travel destination because to its excellent infrastructure and tourist-friendly amenities.

While Tamarindo boasts stunning beaches and a vibrant ambiance, it has had several difficulties due to overdevelopment and environmental effect. These problems are being addressed, and the region is trying to encourage eco-friendly tourism methods.

In general, Tamarindo is a well-liked vacation spot in Costa Rica for beach lovers, surfers, and those looking for an exciting and energetic getaway.

8. **La Fortuna Waterfall**:

A well-known tourist destination in Costa Rica is the La Fortuna Waterfall, which is close to the town of La Fortuna. Visitors come from all over the world to see it since it is one of the most beautiful waterfalls in the nation.

The waterfall is located in the renowned Arenal Volcano National Park, which is home to diverse species, lush jungles, and the magnificent Arenal Volcano. The Arenal River's flow, which rushes over a rock for 70 meters (230 feet), forms the waterfall, which is a beautiful sight.

Visitors must trek a trail that descends through the woods in order to reach La Fortuna Waterfall. Depending on your pace and degree of fitness, the hike takes 20 to 30 minutes. You can take in the surrounding area's natural splendor, including a variety of plant types and the sounds of tropical birds, while you travel.

When you arrive at the trail's end, you will find a sizable pool of water where you can cool yourself by swimming. The water is refreshing and chilly, providing a welcome break from the tropical heat. However, for safety considerations, swimming is only permitted in specific locations.

Be aware that the trek back up may be difficult due to the frequent stair climbs. It's crucial to pace yourself appropriately, bring drink, and wear comfortable shoes. Additionally, be prepared for the chance of coming across slick paths because of the waterfall's mist. For those who enjoy the outdoors and adventure, visiting La Fortuna Waterfall is an excellent experience. It offers the chance to experience the unadulterated splendor of Costa Rica's natural landscapes and to go on an unforgettable trip deep within the rainforest.

9. **Montezuma:**

Montezuma is a popular tourist destination located in the Costa Rica's Puntarenas Province. It is a tiny village located along the gorgeous Pacific coast of the nation at the southernmost point of the Nicoya Peninsula. Beautiful beaches, luxuriant tropical trees, and a vibrant bohemian vibe are all hallmarks of Montezuma.

The breathtaking coastline of Montezuma, which has beautiful white sand beaches, turquoise oceans, and rocky coves, is one of the city's main draws. The town's primary beach, Playa Montezuma, is a fantastic location for swimming, tanning, and taking part in water sports like kayaking and snorkeling. It's also worthwhile to visit nearby beaches like Playa Grande and Playa Las Manchas.

Along with its natural beauty, Montezuma provides a variety of outdoor activities and excursions. Visitors can explore the neighboring Cabo Blanco Nature Reserve, which is home to a variety of species, hiking paths, and a lovely beach. It was Costa Rica's first national park. Another well-liked site is the Montezuma Waterfalls, which are close to the town.

These waterfalls offer swimming and cliff jumping opportunities due to their cascading nature.

The town center of Montezuma exudes a carefree, bohemian charm. It has a wide selection of unique eateries, cafes, and pubs that serve both regional and global food. Additionally, visitors can browse the boutique stores and art galleries that feature the creations of regional artisans and painters.

Overall, Montezuma is a great vacation spot for folks who enjoy the outdoors, outdoor activities, and calm beach vacations. It is a well-liked destination among visitors to Costa Rica due to its blend of natural beauty, outdoor activities, and dynamic environment.

10. Rio Celeste

Costa Rica is home to the lovely natural beauty known as Rio Celeste. It is renowned for having a magnificent turquoise-blue hue that results from a special admixture of minerals and sunshine that seeps into the water.

The Tenorio Volcano National Park, which is in Costa Rica's province of Alajuela, contains the river. It provides tourists with the opportunity to explore the amazing biodiversity of the nation and is surrounded by a lush rainforest.

The "Catarata del Rio Celeste" waterfall is one of Rio Celeste's most notable features. A beautiful pool is below where the waterfall descends from a height of around 30 meters (98 ft). Hikers can use the park's pathways to travel to the waterfall and take in its captivating beauty.

The "Teideros," or locations where two rivers converge and provide the distinctive blue tint, are another noteworthy aspect of Rio Celeste. Minerals like calcium carbonate and copper sulfate, which reflect sunlight and give the water its distinct color, are responsible for this phenomena.

Joining a tour group or hiring a local guide who is knowledgeable about the park, its species, and the area before visiting Rio Celeste is advised. Wearing the proper footwear is crucial because the paths can be slick and muddy. To maintain the river's natural nature, swimming is also not permitted there.

Rio Celeste is a Costa Rican natural marvel that provides tourists with the opportunity to see the country's rich natural history and behold a truly stunning sight.

11. Manuel Antonio Beach.

It is a section of the famed Manuel Antonio National Park, known for its astounding biodiversity and breathtaking scenery. Here are some details on Manuel Antonio Beach:

- Location: Manuel Antonio Beach is located about 132 kilometers (82 miles) southwest of the nation's capital, San Jose, in the Puntarenas Province of Costa Rica.
- Beautiful scenery: The beach is renowned for its gorgeous white sand, blue waves, and lush surrounds. It has stunning views of the Pacific Ocean and a lush rainforest encircling it.
- The beach is located inside the confines of Manuel Antonio National Park, which has an approximate 16.7 square kilometer area (6.4 square miles). Monkeys, sloths, iguanas, and various bird species are among the diverse animals that call the park home.
- Visitors at Manuel Antonio Beach have a variety of outdoor activities at their disposal. Tourists enjoy swimming, sunbathing, and snorkeling. Additionally, there are chances for hiking, wildlife viewing, and nature trail exploration in the nearby jungle.
- The extraordinary biodiversity of Manuel Antonio National Park is well-known. It is a top destination for those who love the outdoors because it includes both marine and terrestrial environments. Numerous endangered animal species live in the park, which also has a variety of plant types.
- Regulations for the Park: In order to maintain the natural integrity of the park, there are rules in place, such as visiting limits and prohibitions on carrying food into specific sections. To assist in preserving the delicate ecosystem of the park, abide by these rules strictly.

- o Accessibility: The village of Quepos is close to Manuel Antonio Beach. To go to the beach and the national park, there are taxis and public buses available.
- o Accommodations and Services: A variety of lodging options are available in the neighborhood, including hotels, resorts, and eco-lodges. To meet the demands of guests, there are also nearby restaurants, stores, and tour operators.

It is advised to carry sunscreen, insect repellent, and good walking shoes when visiting Manuel Antonio Beach. To preserve the preservation of this natural wonderland, keep in mind to adhere to the park's rules and regulations.

12. Rincon de la Vieja National Park

The following are some of its main characteristics.

- Biodiversity: With a diverse range of vegetation and fauna, the national park is famous for its rich biodiversity. Over 300

species of birds, animals, reptiles, and amphibians can be discovered among the different habitats that can be found inside the park, which includes both tropical rainforests and dry woods.
- Hiking Paths: Visitors can experience its natural splendor on a number of well-maintained hiking trails. There are alternatives for both casual walkers and more experienced hikers on the paths, which range in length and difficulty. Beautiful waterfalls, active volcanoes, and an abundance of wildlife may all be found along the routes.
- La Cangreja Waterfall, Escondida Waterfall, and Oropendola Waterfall are just a few of the stunning waterfalls that can be seen in the park. These cascades provide beautiful scenery and cool swimming holes.
- Hot Springs and Mud Pots: The volcanic activity here provides a rare opportunity for visitors to take advantage of hot springs and mud pots, where they can unwind in naturally occurring thermal pools of varying temperatures and indulge in mud baths, which are thought to have therapeutic properties.
- Adventure Activities: The park provides a variety of adventure activities, including horseback riding, whitewater rafting, and canopy tours (zip-lining). Visitors can view the park's natural marvels from a new angle thanks to these activities.
- Facilities for Visitors: it offers amenities for visitors, such as a visitor center, restrooms, and picnic spots. Within the park's specified

sections, camping is also permitted, but you should check the rules and availability in advance.

Please be aware that exact facts and circumstances are subject to change, so it is always advised to check the most recent information from official sources or regional tour operators before making travel arrangements.

13.Cahuita National Park

The magnificent environmental preserve known as Cahuita National Park is located on Costa Rica's Caribbean coast. The area is well known for its stunning beaches, vibrant coral reefs, and diverse wildlife. The following information about Cahuita National Park:

- Cahuita National Park is situated in the province of Limón on Costa Rica's southeast coast. Its total area is roughly 2,732 acres (1,106 hectares) of land and 22,400 acres (9,067 hectares) of sea.

- Biodiversity: The park is renowned for its rich biodiversity, both on land and in the sea. Many ecosystems, including coral reefs, mangroves, and rainforests, are protected by it. Visitors can witness howler monkeys, sloths, toucans, reptiles, and a variety of aquatic animals, including colorful fish, sea turtles, and even dolphins.
- Routes for Hiking: There are numerous well-maintained hiking trails where visitors can explore Cahuita National Park's breathtaking natural beauty. The most popular route is an 8-kilometer (5-mile) coastline walk that travels beside the park's beautiful beaches and offers breathtaking views of the Caribbean Sea. While trekking, you can observe wildlife and hear the sounds of nature.
- Snorkeling and diving enthusiasts will find Cahuita to be a paradise thanks to the park's coral reefs, which are a major feature. The coral reefs are a part of the Mesoamerican Barrier Reef System, the second-largest barrier reef in the world. While scuba divers can venture further out to witness the incredible marine life, which includes sea turtles, tropical fish, and coral with vivid colors, snorkelers can explore the shallow waters near the coast.
- Cahuita National Park has tourist facilities to enhance the experience of visitors. Near the park's entrance is a visitor center providing details on the ecology of the area and admittance requirements. Additional picnic sites and camping places are available for visitors who want to stay longer in the park.

- Attempts at conservation The preservation of the region's natural riches depends on the park. It aims to protect and preserve the diverse habitats, including rainforests, mangroves, and coral reefs. Cahuita National Park collaborates with local communities and organizations to promote environmentally friendly practices and raise awareness of the need of conservation.

A wonderful opportunity to experience Costa Rica's natural splendor, learn about its different ecosystems, and see a variety of species, both on land and underwater, is to visit Cahuita National Park. This national park offers a wonderful experience for anyone who loves the outdoors, whether they are a hiker, snorkeler, or both.

13. Irazú Volcano

In Costa Rica, Central America, there is an active volcano called the Iraz Volcano. It is one of the most well-known and popular natural attractions in the nation. Here are some details regarding the Iraz Volcano:

- Location: The Iraz Volcano is found in Costa Rica's Central Highlands, some 31 kilometers (19 miles) northeast of the nation's capital, San José. It is a section of the approximately 5,705 hectare Iraz Volcano National Park (14,088 acres).
- Despite the fact that its most recent significant eruption took place in 1963, the Iraz Volcano is still considered to be active. It has erupted intermittently ever since, with smaller eruptions in 1994 and 1996. Within its main crater, the volcano's ongoing gas and steam emissions have formed a remarkable crater lake.
- Crater Lake: Diego de la Haya is a greenish-gray crater lake located in the Iraz Volcano's main crater. Depending on the mineral concentration and volcanic activity, the lake's color might change. From lookout spots and trails in the national park, visitors can observe the crater lake.
- Iraz Volcano is a well-liked day trip destination for visitors and locals due to its accessibility by road from San José. Before arriving at the park's entrance, the meandering road takes travelers past beautiful vistas and cloud forests.
- Views: The peak of the Iraz Volcano gives stunning panoramic views of the surroundings on clear days. The Central Valley, the Pacific Ocean, and even the Caribbean Sea are all visible from the top.

- Parking lots, picnic spaces, restrooms, and walking trails are just a few of the visitor amenities available in the Iraz Volcano National Park. It is crucial to note that the weather at the peak can be chilly and windy due to the height, thus it is advised to pack suitable clothing.
- Iraz Volcano has cultural significance for Costa Ricans because of its historical relevance. It erupted in 1963 on the same day that American President John F. Kennedy was in the nation. His trip to the volcano had to be canceled due to the eruption, but both locals and visitors were still affected.

The Iraz Volcano gives a singular opportunity to experience Costa Rica's breathtaking natural beauty and geological mysteries. However, because volcanic activity can change over time, it's crucial to check with local authorities or tour companies for the most up-to-date information on safety and access.

14. Santa Teresa

On the Nicoya Peninsula in Costa Rica, Santa Teresa is a well-known beach town. It's renowned for its gorgeous coastline, reliable surf breaks, and laid-back vibe. Santa Teresa, which is located in the country's northwest, is a part of the larger Puntarenas province.

The town was formerly a modest fishing community that over time underwent a dramatic transformation into a popular tourist attraction. Travelers from a variety of backgrounds are drawn there, including families seeking a quiet beach break, hikers, yoga enthusiasts, and surfers.

Santa Teresa's immaculate beaches are one of its key attractions. Long lengths of white sand in this location are bordered by palm trees that wave in the wind. The area's major beach, Playa Santa Teresa, is a sanctuary for surfers with great conditions for all skill levels. Visitors also enjoy visiting nearby beaches including Playa Hermosa and Playa Carmen.

Santa Teresa is renowned for its thriving yoga and wellness scene in addition to its surfing. There are numerous yoga retreats and studios in the region that provide a variety of lessons and workshops. It's the perfect spot to unwind and regenerate because of the calm and beautiful surroundings.

Santa Teresa exudes a carefree, bohemian attitude. Small hotels, coastal homes, and inviting restaurants serving delectable foreign and regional cuisine are scattered throughout the town itself. Additionally, there are bars and nightclubs where guests may take in live music and meet other travelers.

Santa Teresa has a variety of options for exploration and adventure in addition to beach activities. Visitors can try their hand at stand-up paddleboarding in the calm coastal waves, go horseback riding along the shore, and take ATV rides to surrounding waterfalls and wildlife parks.

The most common method of transportation to Santa Teresa is a combination of methods. Tambor Airport, which is roughly a 45-minute drive away, is the closest airport. An alternative is to arrive in San José's Juan Santamara International Airport and then go to Santa Teresa via bus, shuttle, or domestic flight.

Overall, Santa Teresa is a charming coastal town in Costa Rica that provides a mix of unspoiled landscapes, outdoor pursuits, and a relaxed way of life. It is now a sought-after location for surfers, yogis, and tourists looking for a laid-back beach getaway in a breathtaking tropical setting.

16.Cartago

It served as the nation's capital until 1823, when San José took its position. As the first permanent Spanish settlement in Costa Rica, Cartago is renowned for its historical significance. It was founded in 1563.

The city is surrounded by mountains and lush valleys and is located in Costa Rica's Central Valley. About 25 kilometers to the east of San José, the current capital, is where it is situated. Numerous significant historical and cultural landmarks may be found in Cartago, which has a strong colonial background.

The Basilica of Our Lady of the Angels (Basilica de Nuestra Seora de los ngeles) is a notable monument in Cartago. It is a popular destination for pilgrims from Costa Rica and is thought to contain a modest statue of the Virgin Mary. Because of earthquakes, the basilica, which was constructed in the 17th century, has been restored numerous times.

The Santiago Apostle Parish Ruins (Ruinas de la Parroquia Santiago Apóstol) are another noteworthy landmark in Cartago. The colonial church's remnants here were left behind after it was devastated by an earthquake in 1910. The city's past may be seen in the ruins, which are also a favorite destination for tourists.

Additionally, Cartago has a thriving local culture with a number of celebrations and customs. The Romera, which occurs every year in August, is one of the most well-known occasions. Thousands of Costa Ricans walk to the Basilica of Our Lady of the Angels during this pilgrimage as an act of devotion.

Overall, Costa Rica's historic city of Cartago provides a window into the colonial past of the nation. It is a popular tourist destination due to its historical significance, religious sites, and scenic beauty.

17.Heredia and Granada

The cities of Heredia and Granada in Costa Rica provide a great combination of adventure, natural beauty, and cultural attractions. You can use the following information to plan your trip:

Heredia: Just a few miles to the north of San Jose, the country's capital, is the bustling city of Heredia. It is referred to as the "City of Flowers" and boasts colonial buildings, lovely parks, and a bustling central market. The following highlights:

- The heart of the city, Heredia Central Park, is a magnificent park with a lovely fountain, benches, and greenery. A fantastic location to unwind and take in the atmosphere of the neighborhood.
- El Fortn is a medieval stronghold that was built in the eighteenth century and is now a museum. It gives sweeping views of the city and information about Heredia's past.
- Costa Rica is known for its coffee, and Heredia is a great location to learn about the preparation of coffee. Visit Café Britt for a tour to learn about the process from bean to cup and to sip on some delectable coffee.

A four-hour trip north of Heredia is the colonial city of Granada in the neighboring country of Nicaragua. Despite not being in Costa Rica, it is a well-liked side excursion for tourists traveling through the area because of its historical significance and stunning architecture. Here are a few things to do in Granada:

- Parque Central: Surrounded by vibrant colonial structures, cafes, and stores, the central square is the beating heart of Granada. Enjoy the lively environment while strolling.
- La Calzada Street: There are cafes, bars, and businesses lining this pedestrian street close to Parque Central. It's a terrific location for

dining, live entertainment, and souvenir shopping.
- Isletas de Granada: Explore the Isletas, a group of tiny islands created by a volcanic explosion, by boat on Lake Nicaragua. Take in the beautiful scenery, identify wildlife, and discover the culture of the area.

Please be aware that crossing into Nicaragua is required to get from Heredia to Granada, so be careful to check the most recent requirements and make sure you have the required documentation.

18.Cano Negro National Wildlife Refuge

Visits to Costa Rica's Cano Negro National Wildlife Refuge promise to be amazing opportunities to experience the nation's extensive biodiversity. Here are some details to aid you in making your visit plans:

- The Cano Negro National Wildlife Refuge is located in northern Costa Rica, close to the Nicaraguan border. It is a portion of the Arenal Huetar Norte Conservation Area and has a total area of about 9,969 hectares (24,640 acres).
- Biodiversity: The refuge is well-known for the variety of animals it is home to, especially bird species. Over 350 different bird species depend on it as a key habitat, including the magnificent jabiru stork, herons, egrets, kingfishers, and several migratory birds. In the refuge, you might also see caimans, turtles, monkeys, sloths, and other species.
- Rivers, lagoons, and marshes make to the wetland ecosystem that makes up most of Cano Negro. The Rio Frio and Rio Cano Negro

meet at the refuge, creating a network of streams that support a distinctive environment.
- Activities: A narrated boat excursion through the wetlands is the main thing to do at Cano Negro. These tours offer a chance to see wildlife up close and often take a few hours. Your knowledgeable guides will point out and identify various species while sharing information about the ecology of the area. Through approved routes, it's also feasible to walk around and discover the surroundings.
- Ideal Season to Visit: The optimum time to visit Cano Negro is typically thought to be during the dry season, which runs from December to April. Water levels are lower during this time, and wildlife tends to congregate near the last remaining water sources, making it simpler to see animals and birds. The refuge is still open, though, and the lush green scenery has its own allure during the rainy season (May to November).
- Access and lodging: Los Chiles, the hamlet that serves as the refuge's entrance, is the closest one to Cano Negro. San Jose, the Costa Rican capital, is about a three-hour journey from Los Chiles. You can book boat cruises or employ a guide to tour Cano Negro from Los Chiles. In Los Chiles, there are a few other places to stay, including hotels and lodges.

To prepare for a trip to see wildlife, don't forget to carry binoculars, insect repellant, cozy clothes, and sturdy shoes. To preserve the preservation of the delicate environment, always adhere to your guide's recommendations and observe the refuge's laws.

19.Guanacaste

A gorgeous province in Costa Rica, Guanacaste is well-known for its magnificent beaches, national parks, and thriving biodiversity. Guanacaste offers activities for all interests, including natural exploration, outdoor adventure, and beach relaxation. To help you make the most of your visit, consider the following suggestions:

- Discover the beaches: Guanacaste has some of Costa Rica's most unspoiled coastline. Popular alternatives with clean waters and golden sands are Playa Conchal, Playa Flamingo, and Tamarindo. To explore the aquatic world, you can go snorkeling or diving or simply rest, swim, or surf.
- Visit national parks: Santa Rosa and Rincon de la Vieja National Parks are two well-known parks in Guanacaste. There are hiking paths, waterfalls, hot springs, and opportunities to see wildlife in Rincon de la Vieja. The historical significance of Santa Rosa National Park and the abundance of animals, such as howler monkeys and sea turtles, are well known.
- Visit the Arenal Volcano: Despite not being in Guanacaste, this adjacent attraction is a must-

see. You may go on hikes around the volcano, relax in hot springs, and engage in a variety of outdoor pursuits like horseback riding, white-water rafting, and zip-lining.
- Enjoy adventure sports: Guanacaste has a lot to offer those who love the outdoors. You can try your hand at surfing the Pacific waves, go zip-lining through the forest canopy, go on an ATV excursion, or ride a horse along the beach.
- Visit the little villages of Guanacaste, including the province's capital Liberia and Nicoya, to experience the local culture, sample traditional Costa Rican food, and learn about the history of the area.
- Guanacaste is brimming with fauna and incredible natural treasures. To see monkeys, sloths, exotic birds, and other amazing animals, think about going on a wildlife trip. You can also wander through Palo Verde National Park and take in the diverse wetland ecosystems there.
- Enjoy water sports: Guanacaste's coastal regions provide fantastic chances for water sports like sailing, fishing, scuba diving, and snorkeling. To explore surrounding islands, including the Catalina Islands or the Gulf of Papagayo, you can go on a boat cruise.

20. San Jose

The capital and largest city of Costa Rica is San Jose, which is renowned for its thriving culture, historical sites, and picturesque surroundings.

Visit the National Museum of Costa Rica and the Gold Museum, explore the city's ancient buildings, and meander through bustling markets like the Central Market while you're in San Jose. La Sabana Metropolitan Park and the Lankester Botanical Garden are just a couple of the lovely parks and gardens in the city that are worth visiting.

San Jose's strategic location makes it an ideal starting point for day visits to local sights. Visit the Braulio Carrillo National Park, the Poas Volcano National Park, take a coffee farm tour, or travel to the nearby town of Sarchi, which is famed for its traditional crafts.

Some Hidden gems

3. Cerro Chirripó, Costa Rica's tallest peak, is located in the Chirripó National Park, which also provides strenuous walks through cloud forests and rewarding panoramic views from the top.

4. Puerto Viejo de Sarapiqui, a small hamlet in the northeastern section of the nation, serves as a gateway to the rainforest and provides opportunities to go river rafting, take animal tours, and discover the area's abundant biodiversity.
5. Playa Avellanas: This undeveloped beach in Guanacaste Province is well-known among surfers for its huge waves and the well-known "Little Hawaii" surf break.
6. Samara Beach: On the Nicoya Peninsula, Samara is a tranquil and less busy beach town that offers quiet waves, white sands, and a welcoming local vibe.
7. Turrialba is a lovely village tucked away in the Central Valley, surrounded by rolling hills and coffee plantations. With sports like whitewater rafting, canyoning, and mountain biking, it's the perfect location for adventure seekers. The Turrialba Volcano, an active stratovolcano with hiking paths and stunning vistas, is another option for exploration.
8. Drake Bay: A remote paradise renowned for its immaculate beaches and diverse marine life, Drake Bay is situated on the Osa Peninsula in Costa Rica's southwest. It's a great location for dolphin watching cruises, scuba diving, and snorkeling.
9. On the Nicoya Peninsula, the Cabo Blanco Absolute Natural Reserve is home to beautiful hiking routes that wind through a tropical dry forest and out to quiet beaches.
10. National Park of Tapanti: This lesser-known park close to Cartago is a refuge for birdwatching and trekking and features cloud forests, rivers, and beautiful waterfalls.

11. Palo Verde National Park: With an abundance of waterfowl, including the majestic Jabiru stork, this wetland area is a great spot for birdwatching.
12. Playa Conchal: This beach is ideal for swimming and sunbathing and is renowned for its distinctive sand coastline made of crushed seashells.
13. Park National Santa Rosa: This park is home to significant historical buildings including the Hacienda Santa Rosa and the La Casona, in addition to gorgeous beaches and a wide variety of fauna.
14. The Orosi Colonial Church, one of Costa Rica's oldest churches, is located in the gorgeous Orosi Valley, which is also home to hot springs and coffee plantations.
15. Carara National Park is a haven for birdwatchers and is home to scarlet macaws. It is situated between the southwest's dry forests and the southeast's rainforests.
16. Los Quetzales National Park is located in the Talamanca Mountains and is renowned for its beautiful cloud forests. It is also a great place to hike and view wildlife, such as the elusive quetzal.
17. Known for its outstanding scuba diving prospects, Cocos Island is a secluded and undeveloped island that is a UNESCO World Heritage Site.
18. The Marino Ballena National Park is located in the little seaside town of Uvita, where you can see the "Whale's Tail," a distinctive sandbar formation.
19. San Gerardo de Dota is a quaint community tucked away in a cloud forest and a sanctuary for birdwatchers, especially those hoping to see the magnificent quetzal.
20. Barra Honda National Park: This area of the park is renowned for its limestone caves, which you

may enter on a guided trip and which have striking stalactite and stalagmite formations.

Costa Rica Wildlife

The extraordinary biodiversity and abundant fauna of Costa Rica are well known. Numerous plant and animal species can find a home in the nation's different ecosystems, which include coastal areas, mangrove swamps, cloud forests, and rainforests. The following are a some of the famous wildlife species that you can see in Costa Rica:

1. Howler Monkeys: There are four different species of howler monkeys in Costa Rica, and they are distinguished by their boisterous calls that resound through the jungles.

2. Sloths: Both two-toed and three-toed sloths, renowned for their leisurely gait and arboreal lifestyle, can be found in Costa Rica.
3. Toucans: The cloud forests and rainforests of Costa Rica are home to a variety of colorful birds with huge, vivid beaks.

4. Scarlet Macaws: In some areas of Costa Rica, you can witness scarlet macaws flying and feeding. They are distinguished by their distinctive red, blue, and yellow plumage.
5. Resplendent Quetzal: The Costa Rican cloud forests are home to the resplendent quetzal, one of the most stunning birds in the world.

6. Poison Dart Frogs: The poisonous skin of these little, vividly colored frogs is well recognized. Poison dart frogs come in a variety of kinds in

Costa Rica, each with its own distinctive pattern and coloring.
7. Jaguars: Although they are elusive and hardly ever observed, jaguars are still able to be discovered in the wild in some nations, including Costa Rica. They live in isolated places like Corcovado National Park.
8. Sea turtles: Costa Rica's coastlines are home to a number of sea turtle species, including green, hawksbill, and leatherback turtles.

9. Dolphins and whales: Several species of dolphins and whales, including bottlenose dolphins, spinner dolphins, and humpback whales, frequent the waters near Costa Rica.
10. Spider monkeys can be seen swinging among the treetops in Costa Rica's woods. They are renowned for their agility and long limbs.
11. Coatis: The national parks and woods of Costa Rica are frequently home to these raccoon-like creatures with long snouts and striped tails.

12. Tapirs: The distant rainforest regions of Costa Rica are home to the Baird's tapir, the biggest land animal in Central America.
13. Crocodiles: American crocodiles can be seen during boat trips and wildlife excursions in Costa Rica's rivers and mangroves.
14. Butterflies: Costa Rica is home to a wide variety of colorful and intricately patterned butterfly species. There are numerous butterfly gardens and reserves where you can get a close-up look.
15. Ocelots and margays are two diminutive wild cats that live in Costa Rica's deep jungles and are distinguished by their stunningly speckled hair.

These are just a few illustrations of the amazing wildlife that you can see in Costa Rica. The nation is a haven for many species thanks to its dedication to conservation and protected areas, making it a haven for those who enjoy the outdoors and animals.

Activities to do as a family during a trip to Costa Rica

Families can engage in a variety of activities in Costa Rica. Here are a few well-liked choices:

- Visit national parks to experience amazing wildlife, wander through nature, and take in the landscape. Two excellent choices are Manuel Antonio National Park and Arenal Volcano National Park.
- Zip-lining: Take the whole family on an exhilarating zip-line trip through the rainforest canopy, which offers breath-taking views and an adrenaline rush.
- Take a guided trip to see rare wildlife species like monkeys, sloths, toucans, and others in their natural settings.

- White-water rafting: The rivers of Costa Rica provide thrilling white-water rafting experiences that are ideal for people of all ages and skill levels. Enjoy a day on the water that is exciting and fun.
- Lessons in surfing: If your family enjoys water sports, consider taking lessons in surfing together. Both novice and expert surfers will find great beaches in Costa Rica.
- Canopy tours: Enjoy the thrill of a canopy tour as you go through platforms, hanging bridges, and zip lines while taking in expansive vistas of the jungle.
- Visit a hot spring: Rejuvenate and relax in the hot springs that are found nearby Arenal Volcano. The entire family will enjoy the calming effects of these warm, mineral-rich waters.
- Exploring Costa Rica's diverse marine life when snorkeling or scuba diving. Coral reefs of various colors and different fish species can be found in the seas around the coast.
- Take a tour of a cacao plantation to learn more about the world of chocolate. Sample some delectable chocolate while learning about the production process.
- Riding a horse: Take a ride on the beach, across the countryside, or along gorgeous pathways. It's a wonderful opportunity to discover Costa Rica's sceneries and get closer to nature.
- Visit butterfly and hummingbird gardens: Butterfly and hummingbird gardens can be

found all across Costa Rica. As the lovely species fly by, awe at their beauty.
- Discover the cloud woods: For a singular experience amidst misty forests, hanging bridges, and varied flora and fauna, head to Monteverde Cloud Forest Reserve or Santa Elena Cloud Forest Reserve.

Always remember to double-check each activity's suitability requirements, age restrictions, and safety protocols.

Chapter 4:
Itineraries

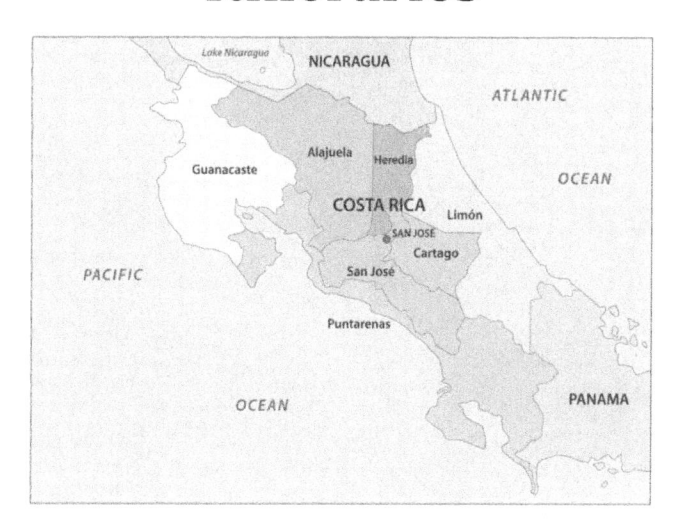

1 Esparza
2 Montes de Oro
3 Quepos
4 Parrita
5 Corredores
6 Garabito
7 Monteverde
8 Puerto Jiménez
9 Corredores

PUNTARENAS

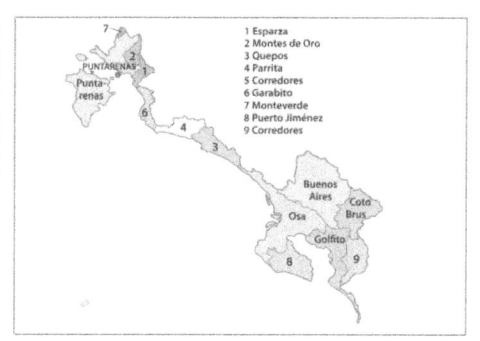

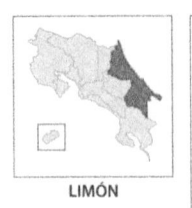

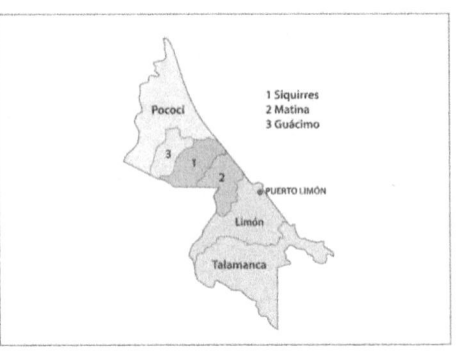

LIMÓN

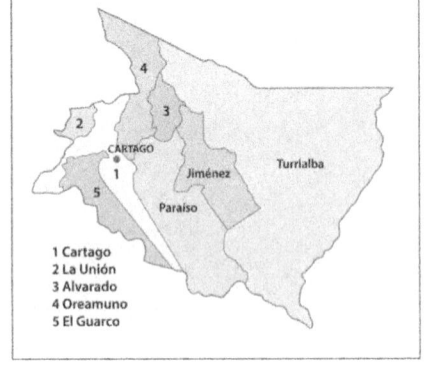

1 Siquirres
2 Matina
3 Guácimo

Pococí
Limón
Talamanca
PUERTO LIMÓN

CARTAGO

1 Cartago
2 La Unión
3 Alvarado
4 Oreamuno
5 El Guarco

Jiménez
Paraíso
Turrialba

SAN JOSÉ

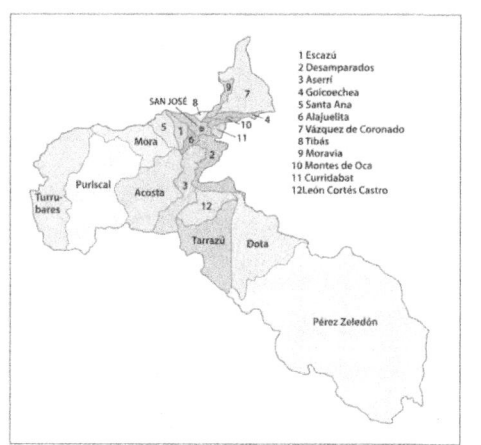

1 Escazú
2 Desamparados
3 Aserrí
4 Goicoechea
5 Santa Ana
6 Alajuelita
7 Vázquez de Coronado
8 Tibás
9 Moravia
10 Montes de Oca
11 Curridabat
12 León Cortés Castro

HEREDIA

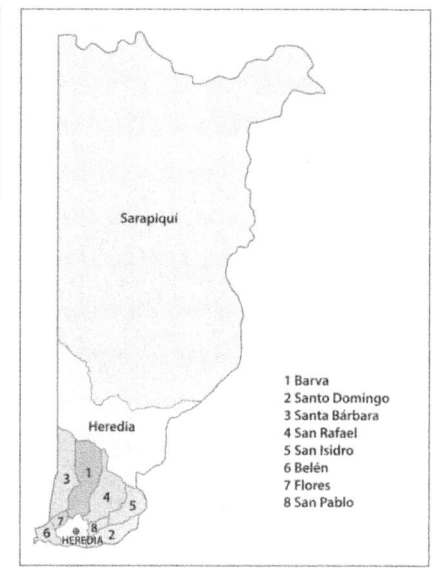

1 Barva
2 Santo Domingo
3 Santa Bárbara
4 San Rafael
5 San Isidro
6 Belén
7 Flores
8 San Pablo

ALAJUELA

1 Alajuela
2 Grecia
3 San Mateo
4 Atenas
5 Naranjo
6 Palmares
7 Poás
8 Orotina
9 Zarcero
10 Sarchí
11 Río Cuarto

GUANACASTE

1 Hojancha

3 days itinerary

Day 1: Exploring San Jose and Cultural Sites

- Morning: Investigate San Jose, the nation's capital, to start the day. Learn about the history and culture of Costa Rica by visiting the National Museum.
- Afternoon: Wander through the bustling Mercado Central (Central Market), where you can savor regional cuisine, purchase trinkets, and take in the energetic ambiance.
- Evening: Spend a laid-back evening indulging in authentic Costa Rican cuisine at one of the city's many restaurants. Try out casado, ceviche, or gallo pinto.

Day 2: Adventure in Arenal Volcano National Park

- Early in the morning, depart towards La Fortuna, which serves as the park's entrance. Take a trek in the park to start your day off well, discovering the lush rainforest and taking in the beautiful volcano views.
- After the hike, head over to the neighboring La Fortuna Waterfall to cool off in the natural pool at the base of the falls. Beautiful tropical flora envelops the waterfall.
- Evening: Unwind and unwind in a nearby natural hot spring. As you relax in the warm, mineral-rich waters while being surrounded by the rainforest, the hot springs offer a healing experience.

Day 3: Beach Time in Manuel Antonio National Park

- Head to Manuel Antonio National Park in the morning, which is renowned for its

magnificent beaches and varied fauna. Hike the park's pathways while keeping an eye out for colorful birds, sloths, and monkeys.
- Afternoon: Take advantage of the park's immaculate beaches in the late afternoon by visiting Playa Manuel Antonio or Playa Espadilla. Take a swim in the clear seas, unwind on the golden sand, and enjoy the warm sunshine.
- Evening: Take a leisurely stroll along the coastline and take in the stunning views as the sun begins to set. Enjoy a seafood meal at a restaurant on the beach while sampling the day's fresh catch.

Five days itinerary

Day 1: San Jose and Cultural Exploration

- Early in the morning, arrive in San Jose, and tour the old town. Visit sites including the Gold Museum, Plaza de la Cultura, and the National Theater.
- Afternoon: Join a tour of the Pre-Columbian Gold Museum to discover more about the native cultures of Costa Rica and their prehistoric gold artifacts.
- Evening: Have dinner at a neighborhood eatery and take in San Jose's exciting nightlife.

Day 2: Arenal Volcano and Hot Springs

- Early in the morning, depart for La Fortuna to see Arenal Volcano National Park. Explore the park's pathways, take in the volcano's enormous presence, and take in the panoramic views by going on a guided hike.

- Afternoon: Rejuvenate and relax at the local hot springs. Choose from a number of resorts that feature hot springs, where you may relax in the mineral-rich, warm water while taking in the tropical ambiance.
- Evening: Have a nice dinner in La Fortuna and think about taking a trip at night to see the lava flows from the volcano (if active).

Day 3: Monteverde Cloud Forest

- Transfer in the morning to the well-known cloud forest destination of Monteverde. Discover the wonderful variety of flora and animals, including several bird species, at the Monteverde Cloud Forest Reserve by hiking through lush trails.
- Visit the Hummingbird Gallery and Butterfly Garden in the afternoon to see and learn about the amazing world of hummingbirds and butterflies.
- Evening: Experience the distinctive sights and sounds of nocturnal wildlife by going on a night stroll in the cloud forest. The woodland can be explored at night on guided tours.

Day 4: Manuel Antonio National Park

- Early in the morning, depart towards the Pacific coast's Manuel Antonio National Park. Investigate the park's pathways and look for animals including monkeys, sloths, and vibrant birds. Bring your bikini to the beach, of course.
- Afternoon: Unwind and take in the stunning beaches found inside the national park. Swim,

sunbathe, or just relax in the stunning coastal environment.
- Evening: Enjoy the sunset from a seaside bar or restaurant. Enjoy delectable seafood dishes while taking in the tranquil beach ambiance.

Day 5: Beach Time and Departure

- Morning: Choose a beach place to spend your final day. Think about visiting Tamarindo, Jaco, or Playa Flamingo, where you can go snorkeling or surfing or just unwind on the sandy beaches.
- Afternoon: Depending on the time of your flight, you might still have a few hours to spend at the beach or finishing up your souvenir shopping.
- Evening: Depart for your next adventure while carrying happy memories of Costa Rica. Transfer to the airport and say goodbye to this lovely nation.

7 days iterary

Day 1: Arrival in San José

- Arrive at San José's Juan Santamara International Airport.
- Get a ride to your hotel and check in.
- Explore the city's cultural and historical sites, such as the National Museum or the Gold Museum.
- Get a good night's sleep after having dinner at a neighborhood eatery.

Day 2: Arenal Volcano and Hot Springs

- Leave for La Fortuna, where the renowned Arenal Volcano is located.
- Enjoy breathtaking views of the volcano and the surroundings by going on a hike around Arenal Volcano National Park.
- Unwind in the natural hot springs, which are known for their healing qualities.
- If you feel adventurous, think about participating in an optional adventure activity like zip-lining or canyoning.
- In La Fortuna, spend the night.

Day 3: Monteverde Cloud Forest

- Travel to the town of Santa Elena, located in the Monteverde Cloud Forest region.
- Embark on a guided tour through the Monteverde Cloud Forest Reserve, known for its diverse flora and fauna.
- Experience the excitement of crossing treetop suspension bridges.
- Visit the butterfly sanctuary and hummingbird garden.
- Sleep over in Monteverde.

Day 4: Manuel Antonio National Park

- Transfer to the Manuel Antonio National Park, which is renowned for its wildlife abundance and spotless beaches.
- Visit the park's paths for a leisurely trek to see monkeys, sloths, and a variety of birds.
- Swim in the clear waters and unwind on one of the park's lovely beaches.
- Enjoy a meal while the sun sets over the water.

- Near Manuel Antonio National Park, spend the night.

Day 5: Manuel Antonio (Free Day)

- Utilize a free day to engage in extracurricular pursuits like kayaking, surfing, or snorkeling.
- Explore the bustling marina in the nearby town of Quepos.
- Enjoy some local seafood at a restaurant.
- Relax and take in the area's stunning scenery.
- Near Manuel Antonio National Park, spend the night.

Day 6: Tortuguero National Park

- Travel to the Caribbean coast's Tortuguero National Park early in the morning.
- Enjoy a beautiful boat trip around the canals while you take in the area's abundant biodiversity.
- Learn about the park's efforts to safeguard endangered species by visiting the sea turtle conservation center (seasonal).
- Discover the relaxed ambiance of Tortuguero village.
- In Tortuguero, stay the night.

Day 7: Return to San José

- Depart from Tortuguero and return to San José.
- Spend the remaining time shopping or continuing your city exploration.
- Visit a nearby restaurant to sample authentic Costa Rican food.
- Sleep in San José.

Two weeks itinerary

Day 1-3: San Jose and Arenal Volcano

- Arrive in Costa Rica's main city of San Jose.
- Visit places like the National Theater and the Gold Museum while spending the day getting to know the city.
- Visit La Fortuna, which is close to the Arenal Volcano, on day two.
- Take part in activities including ziplining, hiking, and hot springs soaking.
- Visit the volcano and its gorgeous surrounds by taking a guided tour.

Day 4-6: Monteverde Cloud Forest

- Visit Monteverde, which is renowned for its breathtaking cloud forests.
- Visit the reserve on a guided hike to see the astounding biodiversity.
- Visit the Monteverde Butterfly Gardens or go on an exhilarating canopy trip.
- Enjoy bird watching while discovering Santa Elena's picturesque town.

Day 7-10: Manuel Antonio National Park and Quepos

- On the Pacific coast, visit Manuel Antonio National Park.
- The park's beaches, hiking paths, and wildlife, including monkeys and sloths, may all be explored in one day.
- Enjoy the gorgeous beaches and the warm waves while you unwind.

- Visit the neighbouring town of Quepos, which is renowned for its lively eateries and energetic environment.

Day 11-13: Tortuguero National Park

- Journey to the Caribbean coast's Tortuguero.
- Visit the park's network of canals by boat to see turtles, caimans, and unusual bird species.
- Learn about the sea turtle conservation initiatives while exploring the community.
- Relax on the remote beaches and see the Tortuguero Museum.

Day 14: Departure

- Go back to San Jose so you can go.
- Continue your city exploration if you have time, or go last-minute souvenir shopping.

Weekend itinerary

Day 1: Arrival and Exploration

Morning:

- Arrive to Costa Rica's capital city of San José's Juan Santamara International Airport.
- Get a taxi or a shuttle to your lodging, then check in.

Afternoon:

- Discover San José for yourself. Visit the Central Market, the Pre-Columbian Gold Museum, and the National Museum.
- Visit a nearby restaurant for a typical Costa Rican meal.

- Explore La Sabana Metropolitan Park, a sizable urban park with paths for walking and entertainment spaces.

Evening:

- Eat dinner at a neighborhood eatery in San José and sample some classic Costa Rican fare.
- To experience the exciting nightlife of the city, think about going to a salsa club or a live music venue.

Day 2: Adventure in Arenal Volcano National Park

Morning:

- Leave San José early and travel to Arenal Volcano National Park in the north (approximately a 3-hour drive).
- Discover the park's hiking routes and enjoy the stunning Arenal Volcano vistas.

Afternoon:

- Visit the rainforest canopy on a thrilling ziplining adventure.
- Baldi or Tabacon hot springs, which are renowned for their calming thermal waters, are great places to soak and unwind.
- At one of the neighborhood eateries close to the park, enjoy a great lunch.

Evening:

- Go back to your lodging near Arenal Volcano and relax.
- To learn more about the unique nocturnal fauna of the jungle, think about signing up for a night trek or a guided wildlife tour.

Day 3: Beach Relaxation in Manuel Antonio National Park

Morning:

- Leave your Arenal lodging and proceed to Manuel Antonio National Park on the Pacific coast (approximately a 4-hour drive).
- When you get to Manuel Antonio, check into the seaside hotel or resort of your choice.

Afternoon:

- Explore the gorgeous beaches of Manuel Antonio National Park. Hike gently along the park's trails to see monkeys, sloths, and a variety of birds.
- Relax on the beautiful white sand beaches and take a refreshing swim in the turquoise waters.

Evening:

- From the beach, take in the magnificent Pacific Ocean sunset.
- Enjoy a seafood supper at a Manuel Antonio restaurant.
- Enjoy the peace and quiet by taking a stroll along the beach at night.

Chapter 5: Where To Stay

You should have a general idea about where you will be staying before you get to Costa Rica, particularly if you will be staying for longer than a month. Besides knowing the specific province or city and address, the most important part about finding suitable accommodations in Costa Rica is knowing what options are available.

Some of the things to consider when looking for a place to stay include your length of stay, the quality of life you expect to have in Costa Rica, and of course - the size of your budget. Generally, a monthly budget of $1,500 will enable two people to live a comfortable life including paying for housing, utilities, food, entertainment, health insurance, with a little left over for savings. In due time, other aspects such as the proximity to your workplace, transport access, and proximity to schools will determine your choice of accommodation in the country.

Here are the best accommodation choices while in the country:

Hostel La Posada - Affordable, Friendly, Beach Vibes

Santa Teresa, Nicoya Peninsula, Puntarenas Province

This international surf camp and hostel sits just a few steps from the infamously beautiful beach of Santa Teresa. The bustling little town of Santa Teresa stretches out over a few miles, hugging the coastline and backed by dense jungle that rises a hill (a great spot to enjoy an aerial view of the sunset and perfect waves stretching out in every direction). As such, it's a very long walk from one side of town to the other.

Hostel La Posada enjoys being right in the center of activity, close to a supermarket, local Soda, surfboard and ATV rentals, and many buzzing local restaurants, bars, and even a few dance clubs.

Lake Arenal Hotel & Brewery (LAB) - Stunning Views, Good Food, Peaceful Nature

Lake Arenal (off the highway near the town of Tilarán), Guanacaste Province

"Good Food. Good Beer. Good Times." That's the simple slogan of this tranquil oasis, and it's more than enough for the weary traveler looking for a peaceful place to set a spell.

While the hotel rooms aren't exactly expensive, they're not necessarily affordable for the budget traveler, either. But, pro tip - ask for a bed in one of their lesser-known cozy dorm rooms! The dorm rooms are often empty, so you might have the place to yourself, plus they feature a fireplace and sliding glass doors to the perfectly manicured lawn and jungle just behind it, and the lake beyond that - first-class accommodation for a dorm room. To top it all off, the staff are warm-hearted and quick with a smile, truly making you feel like you are right at home.

Pura Vida Hostel - Affordable, Great Vibes, Good Music

Tamarindo, Nicoya Peninsula, Guanacaste Province

Pura Vida Hostel stands out for their affordability, cleanliness, friendly vibes from multilingual staff, and best of all - their genuinely chilled out atmosphere and amazing live music and entertainment all week long.

Tranqui Funkey Cabinas

Playa Avellana, Guanacaste Province

Tranqui Funkey is a delightfully designed, hip little surf and yoga village located just 30 minutes south of bustling Tamarindo. It's a wild place, far from the noisy, busy cities, offering beautiful tan sand, mangrove trees providing shade not far from the shore, and crystal-clear waters. There's an open-air kitchen, a very large wooden deck built above the kitchen (with more hammocks) for yoga, meditation, or to simply relax, a BBQ area, flowers everywhere, even a lovely tiny bar and organic restaurant.

Casa Mariposa

San Gerardo de Rivas, San José Province (at the base of Cerro Chirripó)

This is a wonderfully unique and incredibly beautiful lodge nestled in a tiny mountain town, conveniently close to the entrance of Cerro Chirripó National Park and the entrance to Cloudbridge Nature Reserve

Cool Vibes Hostel

Dominical, Puntarenas Province

Their motto is "Stay, Relax, Enjoy," and this is exactly what this hostel offers - cozy, affordable accommodations, very friendly staff for a great price, a huge, shared kitchen and living room, and a tiny pool. Plus, it's only steps away from the beach.

Hotel Casa Tago

Alajuela, San José, San José Province

This lovely little family hotel is an oasis in the busy neighborhoods of Alajuela (a kind of "city-within-a-city" located in San José that is conveniently close to the airport). It has a gorgeous pool, private rooms with flat-screen TVs, free breakfast, and a 24hr front desk

Wide Mouth Frog Hostel

Quepos, Puntarenas Province

This is a well-done little backpackers' hostel in the transit town of Quepos - you'll likely stop here at some point if you travel south along the Pacific Coast. The hostel boasts friendly staff, tropical gardens, a large pool, a shared kitchen, an on-site restaurant, gated grounds, and a lot of good vibes.

Flutterby House

Uvita, Puntarenas Province

This unique place is an eco-friendly hostel with an on-site bar and restaurant. It has a beautiful kitchen and yoga deck

Chapter 6: Costa Rica Cuisine and Restaraunts

Costa Rican cuisine is savory, hearty and never disappoints. Expect generous portions served and freshly brewed coffee as well as colorful fruits at every meal.

Costa Ricans love fresh bread, and it is almost a ritual to visit the bakery every morning to purchase some freshly baked bread. The same goes to fruits and vegetables, weekly trips to the farmer's market for fresh vegetables, fruits and produce are customary in Costa Rica.

Rice and beans are Costa Rica's staples, and they are featured in almost every meal including maize meal in the form of tortillas. Costa Rican meals also feature chicken, pork rinds, eggs, beef joints and chorizo which are several types of pork sausages.

Gallo Pinto is what Costa Ricans refer to as breakfast and it often consists of leftovers from dinner including the staple rice and beans, bell peppers and onions served with scrambled eggs, fried plantains and *quesco fresco* which is fresh cheese.

Casado is lunch comprising yet again the staple rice and beans accompanied by pork chops, fried chicken, stewed beef or tilapia. Sides often include spaghetti, fried plantains known as *patacones*, stewed squash known as *picadillo* and fresh cassava.

Dinner will comprise rice and beans, but it could simply be a meal of rice and chicken. French fries served with pink sauce made from mayo and ketchup (*salas rosada*) may also be served for dinner. There are savory variations of rice and beans served with coconut milk, providing quite the treat.

Fresh sea bass is used to make *Ceviche*, which is one of the country's popular dishes. It is often marinated using lime juice, onions and red peppers and accompanied by chips. This is one of the meals you can find in most restaurants or from roadside food vendors.

The *tres leches,* referring to a three-milk cake, is the country's traditional dessert. Soaking the cake in cream, condensed milk and evaporated milk makes the dessert.

Fruit juices are always readily available given that the country has an abundance of tropical fruits. Some of the varieties you will find include: Sour Guava, referred to as *Cas*, is the Costa Rican native fruit; *Pina,* referring to pineapple; *Sandia,* referring to watermelon; *Mora,* referring to blackberry; and *frutas mixtas,* referring to a fruit punch. *Batido* is the equivalent of a smoothie and when ordering you will be asked '*con leche o agua*' meaning whether you prefer it with milk or water. *Horchata* is a traditional Costa Rican drink made from cinnamon and cornmeal.

Cerveceria de Costa Rica is the country's main brewery and brews 8 beer brands. Imperial beer is a favorite from the brewery, which is a conglomerate of the Florida Ice and Farm Company. The brewery has brewed Imperial since 1924 and they now distribute it to the Grand Cayman, U.S. and Australia. Bavaria (not the one from Holland) is also another favorite beer in the country alongside limejuice referred to as Rock Ice con limon and Heineken.

Here are some restaurants that offer Costa Rican cuisine:

1. Popular local eatery Soda Tapia (San José) is well-known for its authentic Costa Rican cuisine, including ceviche, gallo pinto (rice and beans), and casados (a typical Costa Rican dinner with rice, beans, beef, and plantains).
2. Alma de Amón (San José) is a restaurant that specializes in using local, fresh ingredients to make inventive takes on Costa Rican food. They provide a range of foods, such as chifrijo, olla de carne, and arroz con pollo (rice with chicken) (a dish with rice, beans, pork, and avocado).
3. Located in the picturesque Monteverde cloud forest, Soda Y Vino (Monteverde) offers traditional Costa Rican fare such patacones, plantain-stuffed chicken, and arroz con camarones (rice with shrimp) (fried plantains).
4. El Avion (Manuel Antonio) – This distinctive eatery is located within a C-123 Fairchild freight jet that has been restored. They offer Costa Rican food with a modern touch, featuring meals like casados with seafood, fish with plantains as a crust, and coconut flan for dessert on the menu.
5. Restaurante Silvestre (La Fortuna) – This farm-to-table establishment serves up delectable Costa Rican cuisine produced with fresh, regional ingredients. It is located close to the Arenal Volcano. They offer meals including heart of palm salad, chifrijo, and arroz con camarones.
6. Popular seaside soda (small restaurant) in Jaco, Soda Viquez is noted for its inexpensive prices and

substantial amounts of Costa Rican food such arroz con mariscos (rice with shellfish), ceviche, and casados.

7. Soda Mediterraneo (Tamarindo) - This quaint eatery in Tamarindo combines Costa Rican cuisine with flavors from the Mediterranean. They serve a variety of foods, such as seafood paella, rice-stuffed peppers, and grilled fish with salsa made from tropical fruits.

These are just a few instances of eateries serving Costa Rican food. The best method to find the most recent information on Costa Rica's eating options is to look into local recommendations and read online reviews.

HOW TO SAVE MONEY ON FOOD IN COSTA RICA

One thing that you will appreciate in Costa Rica is that food is quite affordable. However, this is mostly the case when you are buying and cooking your own food. Eating out can be quite costly at times. With a number of restaurants catering to the palates of international guests, the prices can get fairly steep. You can still get a decent low costs meal from a small authentic Costa Rican restaurant referred to as *sodas* and they come highly recommended if you aim at sampling authentic Costa Rican cuisines. Note that some of these eateries are very small and don't have table space. You will get a satisfying complete meal and dessert for $5 to $6. Buy your fruits and vegetables from markets as opposed to supermarkets known as supermercado/mercado and they will be fairly cheap. Most towns have Saturday morning fairs referred to as ferias where you can buy varieties of produce affordably.

Chapter 7: Entertainment And Nightlife In Costa Rica

Costa Rica is not on the global scale when it comes to creative arts and music. That doesn't mean that you can't enjoy some music in Costa Rica; in fact, the rich and diverse cultures add some spice to the music of the country. *Cumbia*, which is dance and music brought from Columbia and Africa, is one of the country's favorites.

Latin music like the *Bachata*, *Salsa* and *Meringue* are also quite popular in the country particularly with the older folk. *Reggeaeton*, that combines aspects of Jamaican dancehall and Reggae and Latin rhythms, is more popular with the younger generations.

The eastern side of the country has a predominant Afro-Caribbean population and Calypso, Reggae, Soca and Rumba music are popular in that area.

Costa Ricans enjoy listening to music from all around the world including Rock music, which is popular among the youth. Television stations from North America are accessible in Costa Rica giving them access to music channels like MTV and an influence of the pop culture.

Some of the country's major festivals that will keep you highly entertained include:

- In January all over the country are the *Fiestas de Palmares*. The fiestas include parades, carnivals, bingo and concerts.

- Every last week of February, the Sun Festival that promotes solar power use is held. The country also celebrates the Maya New Year with fire ceremonies every February 25th.
- Monterverde hosts a music festival running from February through March.
- Rey Curre, a village in the Bourca, hosts Fiestas of Diablos depicting fighting between the Spanish and Indians. It incorporates wooden masks, drum music and dancing, and fireworks in the evening.
- Every 2nd Sunday of March, the country celebrates Oxcart Drivers day referred to as the *Dia del Boyero*. Oxcarts, known as *carretas*, are a Costa Rican historical symbol because they were used to transport coffee beans to Puntarenas from the highlands and Central Valley.
- Playas Chiquita, which is located to the south of Puerto Viejo de Limon, hosts a Caribbean Music Festival running from March through April.
- The Guanacaste Day held to commemorate the annexation of Guanacaste with Costa Rica is celebrated every 25th of July. The celebrations feature folk dances, bull teasing and cattle shows.
- September 15th is the country's Independence Day and it celebrates the independence of Central American countries from the colonial rule of Spain. Paper lanterns made by children illuminate the streets as a nocturnal parade is conducted and the Freedom Torch is carried

from Guatemala on to Costa Rica and on to the Central America colonial capital Cartago.
- The Festival of Corn, *Fiesta del Maiz*, is held on October 13th annually. It features costumes made using husks, silks of corn and grains.
- December is when several celebrations take place to usher in Christmas and the New Year. San Jose gets lit up with decorative lights all over and families compete to design nativity scenes, which goes on well through the 22nd of December. Expect to have a lot of coconut candy known as *melcochas*, eggnog known as *rompope*, boiled corn dough that is stuffed with diverse veggies and meat known as *tamales*, corn liquor known as *chichi,* and the equivalent of mashed potatoes and turkey which is rice with chicken referred to as *Arroz con Pollo*.
- A grand parade with a lot of music and decorative floats marks the commemoration of *Festejos Populares* on the 26th of December. It is held at Zapote, which is an amusement park/fair grounds in San Jose. New Year is marked like a huge community fiesta. Neighbors, who have forged strong bonds growing up together, have an open door policy and freely walk in each others homes joining in on parties.

Nightlife In Costa Rica

Costa Rica provides diverse options when it comes to nightlife activities.

The weekend (Fridays and Saturdays) is usually when people go clubbing in Costa Rica. However, ladies' night or discount nights during the week are not uncommon and Costa Ricans simply love partying.

Some clubs/bars offer drinks at discounted rates before 9p.m., but 10 p.m. to 11 p.m. is when clubs really come into full swing. Closing time varies from one establishment to another, but usually closing time is between 2 a.m. to 4 a.m.

What people wear while out clubbing depends on the weather and most tourists are spotted with shorts, tank tops and flip-flops at clubs near the beach/costal towns. In the Central Valley, the weather tends to get colder at night and club patrons are known to dress more sophisticatedly. A nice dress, good pair of jeans and high heels for the ladies should do in most of the towns. There are some clubs that have dress codes and do not allow shorts, tank tops and hats.

Partying is a group affair in the country, with the exception of ladies night when most people go solo.

A noteworthy tip is that there is a distinct difference between a club and a nightclub in Costa Rica. A club equates to your normal dance club while a nightclub is often a strip club. If you are male and new to Costa Rica, asking for the best nightclub will elicit a couple of laughs.

Costa Ricans love dancing and everyone is welcome to bust their best moves on the dance floor. Some Merengue and Salsa knowledge will go a long way in keeping up with the locals on the dance floor. Costa Rican clubs often play Hip-hop, Merengue, Rock, Reggaeton, Salsa and Cumbia music.

Karaoke is quite popular as well and most towns have karaoke bars. San Jose hosts the best Karaoke clubs with both Spanish and English hits.

It is totally acceptable to ask a woman/man for a dance and Costa Ricans tend to be very direct about their intentions. Costa Rican women are very affectionate and direct as well. They also tend to be very flirtatious and a woman kissing a male colleague on the cheek is quite acceptable in Costa Rica. Costa Rican men talk animatedly with hand gestures and they do not shy away from staring at women. In general, most Costa Ricans still live at home with their families until marriage. Therefore, if the night does progress well couples looking for intimacy would go to the country's love motels referred to as *moteles.* Protection is easily available from grocery stores, bar/club bathrooms, pharmacies and *supermercados*. Some *moteles* also provide them at an extra fee.

Chapter 8: Shopping and Souvenirs in Costa Rica

Shopping in Costa Rica may be fun because there are so many alternatives, from traditional markets to cutting-edge malls. Here are some well-liked shopping areas and suggestions to make the most of your shopping in Costa Rica:

San José: As the nation's capital, San José offers a wealth of shopping options. Get traditional meals, fresh fruit, and local crafts at the Central Market (Mercado Central). There are many shops, boutiques, and shopping malls along the busy shopping areas of Avenida Central and Paseo de los Estudiantes.

Escaz: This upmarket shopping destination is west of San José. A contemporary mall containing designer clothing, electronics, and eateries is called Multiplaza

Escaz. Avenida Escaz is a hip outdoor shopping district with shops, galleries, and restaurants.

Santa Ana: Santa Ana, which is close to Escaz, has more shopping opportunities. Momentum Lindora is a well-known shopping complex featuring many different retailers, including a supermarket, household goods, and clothing. There are more stores and restaurants at the nearby outdoor mall Terrazas Lindora.

Jacó: If you're close to the Pacific coast, Jacó is a well-known beach town with a thriving retail scene. Follow Jacó Walk, a pedestrian-only boulevard dotted with boutiques, cafes, and gift shops. There are apparel stores, surf shops, and local craftsmen selling their handmade goods.

Another coastal community is Tamarindo, which is well-known for its surfing and beach culture. Avenida Central, the main thoroughfare, has a variety of boutiques, surf shops, and gift shops. Jewelry, local art, and beachwear are all available here.

Duty-Free Shopping: Take advantage of duty-free shopping at the international airports if you're flying out of Costa Rica. A variety of goods, including electronics, cosmetics, alcoholic beverages, and tobacco, are available at tax-free pricing.

Remember to compare prices and bargain when shopping in local markets. It's also advisable to keep an eye on your belongings and be cautious of pickpockets in crowded areas.

Souvenirs

Here are some popular items to consider when shopping as souvenirs in Costa Rica:

1. Coffee: The superior quality of Costa Rican coffee is well-known around the world. To savor the robust flavors of Costa Rican coffee at home, look for bags of freshly roasted coffee beans or ground coffee.
2. Handmade goods are widely available in Costa Rica. Look for things like woven linens, ceramics, and wooden carvings. These crafts frequently use conventional patterns and motifs drawn from indigenous civilizations.
3. Traditional Dress: The "guayabera" is the name for the "traditional" Costa Rican outfit. This thin, button-up shirt is available in a variety of colors and is made of cotton or linen. It's a well-liked keepsake and useful piece of apparel for warm areas.
4. Salsa Lizano is a typical condiment in Costa Rican cooking. A range of foods, including the classic gallo pinto, pair well with the acidic and somewhat sweet salsa lizano (rice and beans). Most supermarkets and gift shops carry it.
5. Chocolate: The country of Costa Rica is renowned for its premium chocolate. Look for locally produced chocolate bars, cacao goods, or even go on a chocolate tour to discover how chocolate is made and sample a variety of flavors.
6. T-shirts and accessories sold as souvenirs are popular with tourists. They include hats, keychains, magnets, and T-shirts with Costa Rican phrases or recognizable images. These can be discovered at markets, gift shops, and coastal communities.
7. The manufacture of jade is well-known in Costa Rica. Look for jade bracelets, earrings, and pendants with elaborate designs that highlight the

gem's inherent beauty. Just be sure the sellers you are buying from are reliable.
8. Hammocks: Due to the laid-back atmosphere in Costa Rica, hammocks are a common purchase. Hammocks made of cotton or nylon are available in a variety of sizes and eye-catching hues. They are ideal for bringing a little bit of tropical comfort to your patio or backyard.
9. Traditional Instruments: If you enjoy music, you might want to purchase a handcrafted marimba, a type of xylophone, or a painted oxcart wheel, a representation of Costa Rican folklore.

Conclusion

In conclusion, Costa Rica is a beautiful and diverse country with a rich culture and abundant natural beauty. Whether you're interested in outdoor adventures, cultural experiences, or relaxation and wellness, Costa Rica has something for everyone. By planning and being prepared, you can have a safe and enjoyable trip to Costa Rica. With its friendly locals, stunning landscapes, and diverse range of activities, Costa Rica is a destination that is sure to leave a lasting impression.

Printed in Great Britain
by Amazon